Harvard
Business
Review

ON

WORK AND LIFE
BALANCE

THE HARVARD BUSINESS REVIEW PAPERBACK SERIES

The series is designed to bring today's managers and professionals the fundamental information they need to stay competitive in a fast-moving world. From the preeminent thinkers whose work has defined an entire field to the rising stars who will redefine the way we think about business, here are the leading minds and landmark ideas that have established the *Harvard Business Review* as required reading for ambitious businesspeople in organizations around the globe.

Other books in the series:

Harvard Business Review on Brand Management

Harvard Business Review on Breakthrough Thinking

Harvard Business Review on Business and the Environment

Harvard Business Review on the Business Value of IT

Harvard Business Review on Change

Harvard Business Review on Corporate Governance

Harvard Business Review on Corporate Strategy

Harvard Business Review on Crisis Management

Harvard Business Review on Effective Communication

Harvard Business Review on Entrepreneurship

Harvard Business Review Interviews with CEOs

Harvard Business Review on Knowledge Management

Harvard Business Review on Leadership

Harvard Business Review on Managing High-Tech Industries

Harvard Business Review on Managing People

Harvard Business Review on Managing Uncertainty

Harvard Business Review on Managing the Value Chain

Harvard Business Review on Measuring Corporate Performance

Harvard Business Review on Negotiation and Conflict Resolution

Harvard Business Review on Nonprofits

Harvard Business Review on Strategies for Growth

Harvard Business Review

ON

WORK AND LIFE BALANCE

A HARVARD BUSINESS REVIEW PAPERBACK

The *Harvard Business Review* articles in this collection are available as
individual reprints. Discounts apply to quantity purchases. For information and ordering, please contact Customer Service, Harvard Business
School Publishing, Boston, MA 02163. Telephone: (617) 783-7500 or
(800) 988-0886, 8 A.M. to 6 P.M. Eastern Time, Monday through Friday.
Fax: (617) 783-7555, 24 hours a day. E-mail: custserv@hbsp.harvard.edu.

Library of Congress Cataloging-in-Publication Data
Harvard business review on work and life balance.
     p.   cm. — (The Harvard business review paperback series)
     Includes index.
     ISBN 1-57851-328-6
     1. Work—Social aspects.   2. Quality of life.   3. Work and family.
4. Burn out (Psychology).   I. Title: Work and life balance.   II. Series.
  HD4904.H345   2000
    306.3′6—dc21   99-045199
                                                   CIP

Contents

Harvard Business Review

ON

WORK AND LIFE
BALANCE

Work and Life

The End of the Zero-Sum Game

STEWART D. FRIEDMAN,

PERRY CHRISTENSEN, AND

JESSICA DEGROOT

Executive Summary

MOST COMPANIES VIEW work and personal life as competing priorities in a zero-sum game, in which a gain in one area means a loss in the other. From this traditional perspective, managers decide how their employees' work and personal lives should intersect and often view work-life programs as just so much social welfare. A new breed of managers, however, is trying a new tack, one in which managers and employees collaborate to achieve work and personal objectives to everyone's benefit.

These managers are guided by three principles. The first is to clearly inform their employees about business priorities and to encourage them to be just as clear about personal priorities. The second is to recognize and support their employees as whole people, not only acknowledging but also celebrating their roles outside the office. The third is to continually experiment with the way work gets done, looking for approaches that enhance the organization's performance and allow employees to pursue personal goals.

The managers who are acting on these principles have discovered that conflicts between work and personal priorities can actually be catalysts for identifying inefficiencies at the workplace. For example, one manager and his staff found a way to accommodate the increased workload at their 24-hour-a-day command center while granting the staff more concentrated time off.

So far, these managers have usually been applying the principles without official sanction. But as the business impact of their approach becomes better appreciated, the authors predict, more and more companies will view these leaders as heralds of change.

T HE CONFLICTING DEMANDS of work and personal life have always been with us. People have always had children and elderly parents to care for; they have always pursued hobbies and devoted time to community activities. In the past, many managers dealt with such personal needs summarily: "What you do in the office is our business. What you do outside is your own." It was assumed, too, that employees would put the company's interests first. Work versus personal life, after all, was a zero-sum game.

Have times changed? Yes and no. On one hand, striking demographic shifts, such as the increasing number of women in the workforce, have put more mothers on the job, heightening awareness of work-life issues. New economic forces, such as global competition, have also changed the landscape, creating an unprecedented need for committed employees at a time when loyalty is low in the wake of corporate downsizings. On the other hand, most executives still believe that every time an employee's personal interests "win," the organization pays the price at its bottom line. They consign work-life issues to the human resources department, where the problems are often dealt with piecemeal, through programs such as flextime and paternity leave. Such programs, however, rarely help more than a few employees strike a meaningful, sustainable balance between work and personal life because they do not permeate a company's culture or fundamentally change managers' behavior.

Under the Radar

In recent years, however, we have observed that a small but growing number of managers—many of them flying under the radar of officially sanctioned programs— approach the work-life question differently. They operate under the assumption that work and personal life are not competing priorities but complementary ones. In essence, they've adopted a win-win philosophy. And it appears they are right: in the cases we have studied, the new approach has yielded tangible payoffs both for organizations and for individual employees.

These managers are guided by three mutually reinforcing principles. First, they clarify what is important. That is, they clearly inform their employees about business priorities. And they encourage their employees to be just as clear about personal interests and concerns—to identify where work falls in the spectrum of their overall priorities in life. The objective is to hold an honest dialogue about both the business's and the individual's goals and then to construct a plan for fulfilling all of them.

Second, these managers recognize and support their employees as "whole people," open-mindedly acknowledging and even celebrating the fact that they have roles outside the office. These managers understand that skills and knowledge can be transferred from one role to another and also that boundaries—where these roles overlap and where they must be kept separate—need to be established.

Third, these managers continually experiment with the way work is done, seeking approaches that enhance the organization's performance while creating time and energy for employees' personal pursuits.

The three principles lead to a virtuous cycle. When a manager helps employees balance their work lives with the rest of their lives, they feel a stronger commitment to the organization. Their trust redoubles, and so do their loyalty and the energy they invest in work. Not surprisingly, their performance improves, and the organization benefits. Strong results allow the manager to continue practicing the principles that help employees strike this work-life balance.

In the following pages, we will explore the three principles in more detail and illustrate how managers apply them. The cases are drawn from our research into several dozen U.S.-based companies of varying sizes in a variety of industries, supplemented by over 100 interviews conducted and analyzed by our colleagues at the Wharton Work/Life Roundtable. Each case shows that striking a balance between work and personal life is not the task of the manager alone; rather, it is a process that requires a partnership between the manager and individual employees. Ultimately, all the strategies call for an honest two-sided exchange, as well as a mutual commitment to continual change.

CLARIFY WHAT'S IMPORTANT

In most organizations, employees rarely feel comfortable discussing their personal priorities. They worry that admitting a passion for singing with the local opera company, for instance, will be seen as a lack of passion for work. Such fear is not misguided. Most managers believe—or at least hope—that work is at the top of an employee's list of life priorities. For some, it is. For others, of course, work is just a means to the end of achieving other priorities. These people are often put in the uncomfortable position of having to pretend they care primarily about work-related issues that are actually of secondary importance to them.

The managers who strike a work-life balance with their people cut through the charade about priorities. They make business objectives crystal clear, and they define them in terms of outputs—in terms of results. Simultaneously, they ask employees to identify the important goals, concerns, and demands outside the office that require time and energy. One person might be responsible for his elderly mother's health care, which involves three trips to the hospital each month. Another might be in the process of qualifying for a Gold Star in figure skating. Still another may feel strongly that, at this point in her career, none of her priorities is more important than success at work.

Such a discussion of priorities can take place only in an environment of trust, and the managers who are striking a balance between work and personal life with their employees know that. They do not penalize people for putting personal concerns first or for putting them right alongside work. They do not try to persuade people to give up their extracurricular interests. Rather, they use the information about personal priorities to draw a road map toward a singular destination: business success achieved hand in hand with individual fulfillment.

The fact that these managers define business success in terms of results is key. To them, outcomes matter more than process. To that end, they give their employees specific goals but also great autonomy over how to achieve those goals. That way, the woman who is trying to receive a Gold Star in figure skating can practice in the morning when the rink is empty and rates are lower. She can arrive at work at noon, stay until 5 P.M., and then take unfinished tasks home with her to complete in the evening. To her manager, such a schedule is acceptable as long as she is producing the work her job requires.

Steve, a senior operations executive at a global bank, demonstrates the benefits of putting both business and personal priorities on the table. For many years, Steve was a classic hard-driving boss, given to starting the day with 7 A.M. breakfasts with his staff. He also expected his top people to work as late as he did—sometimes close to 10 P.M.

One of those people was a vice president named Jim. At first, Jim played by Steve's rules, "living at work," as he describes it. Then one weekend, Jim's young son fell and cut his knee. To Jim's shock and dismay, the child refused to let Jim comfort him. Indeed, he treated Jim like a stranger. The event was a turning point. Although fearful for his job, Jim approached Steve and said that he had let slip the single most important priority in his life—a close relationship with his son. He made an offer: "Judge me by the quality of my work, not by the amount of time I spend at the office."

The request clearly disconcerted Steve, but because he valued Jim enormously, he agreed to evaluate Jim's performance based solely on his contributions to the bank's success. Both men then had to change how they got things done. They began to plan their time together more carefully. Their meetings became more focused; they cut down on the length and number of reports and memos they sent to each other and got right to the essentials in their communications. Until that point, Jim had helped Steve prepare for the 7 A.M. staff meetings in the half hour prior to them. Under the new arrangement, Jim briefed Steve the day before; soon, in fact, Jim was routinely skipping the 7 A.M. meetings, and his absence had little or no adverse impact. What's more, Jim was able to leave the office regularly at 5 P.M.

An essential role of a leader is to make sure all priorities are part of the discussion of how to achieve success.

For his part, Steve found that Jim's energy and concentration at work soared. Indeed, having made his business and personal priorities explicit, Jim was able to pay unrelenting attention to key business issues while at work. As a result, his performance improved dramatically. He was rewarded with several promotions, rising quickly through the company's ranks.

In time, Jim went on to run a large credit-card business, and he is currently the chief operating officer of a major manufacturing company. Along the way, clarifying what's important has become a fundamental part of his managerial style. In fact, he is well known throughout his current organization for taking family and personal considerations into account in scheduling both his own time and his employees' time.

Steve recently retired. In his farewell address to the organization after a long and successful career, he noted that his experience with Jim was a milestone in his development as a leader. He learned, he said, the business value of allowing employees to meet personal commitments as they pursue organizational goals. An essential role of a leader is to make sure all priorities are part of the discussion of how to achieve success.

RECOGNIZE AND SUPPORT THE WHOLE PERSON

Most managers know about their employees' personal lives to some extent. They know, for instance, that one person has three children or that another is about to be married. Occasionally, they are aware of people's hobbies or community activities. This kind of incidental knowledge, however, bears little resemblance to the second principle as managers who balance issues of work and personal life practice it. Their understanding of employees is deeper and more detailed. Instead of knowing casual facts about people, and beyond learning about priorities, these managers recognize and support the full range of their people's life roles: not just mother or caretaker, but also volunteer with autistic children, aspiring concert pianist, or passionate golfer.

Why do these managers tune into their employees' roles outside the office? First, being sincerely interested in an employee's personal life creates a bond and, with it, trust—which brings organizational benefits familiar to any manager. Second, identifying the various roles helps these managers tap into the full range of their employees' talents. Third, it is necessary for individuals to understand how their roles relate to one another—where they mesh and where they need to be kept separate—to establish effective boundaries. Establishing the boundaries helps remove distractions, allowing people to be more fully focused on the task at hand. Finally, knowing about an employee's personal life is critical if a manager wants to put the first work-life principle to work, crafting a strategy to meet both business and personal goals.

Just as employees don't usually volunteer details of their personal priorities, neither do they openly offer information about their life roles. Indeed, such revelations are countercultural in most big companies today. That is why managers who adopt this principle demonstrate their commitment to it by acting as role models. They openly discuss the benefits and demands of their own roles outside work. The manager of a 15-person work group at a manufacturing company, for instance, freely discusses the challenges of her role as the head of a blended family. At home, she cares for six preteen children from her previous marriage and her husband's two previous marriages all living under one roof. Not only does she apply her experience resolving conflicts in her own family to settling differences within the work group, but she also openly admits, "Everything I know about negotiation I learned at the dinner table." The manager's honesty about her roles as a mother and stepmother invites her employees to be similarly candid about their personal roles.

Another way managers recognize and support the whole person is by valuing the knowledge and skills employees bring to the business from their lives outside work. In one company we studied, for example, a manager named José found out that one of his key sales representatives, Sally, was intensely dedicated to her alma mater, a Big Ten university. She was an active fund-raiser for the school and often used her free time to recruit local high-school students.

After receiving Sally's permission, José called the company's recruiting director. He described Sally's knowledge of and commitment to her alma mater and asked if it would be possible to get her assigned as the company's liaison in its recruiting efforts at the school. As it happened, the company had been having limited success at the school, and the recruiting director was looking for ways to both improve the company's reputation on campus and increase the number of students it was able to recruit, particularly for the sales force. The recruiting director welcomed the chance to talk with Sally, and they met soon thereafter.

The recruiting director was impressed with Sally's energy, ideas, and the relationships she had already forged with the university. He offered her the position of liaison, a task that would likely take up to 20% of her time for half the year. She would replace another sales rep—an individual without personal ties to the school—who was currently doing the job. Sally brought the liaison proposal to José who, despite the fact that it would mean that Sally would spend less time with her customers, recognized the business value of increasing the organization's ability to hire more sales reps from the university.

Conflicts between work and personal priorities can be catalysts for identifying work inefficiencies.

Why did he agree? First, he correctly anticipated that because of her feelings about the school, Sally would do a great job, and her relationship would bear fruit in the company's recruiting effort. Second, he accurately predicted that the loss of Sally's time with customers in the short term would be minimal since she was already spending some of her discretionary time on school events. Finally, José expected that Sally would be grateful for this opportunity to combine her interest in the school with her work. And she was. Sally told us that after she received the liaison position, her commitment to the company skyrocketed. As often is the case, exercising the principle of recognizing and supporting the whole person benefited not just the individual but the company as well.

CONTINUALLY EXPERIMENT WITH THE WAY WORK IS DONE

Most managers in today's rapidly changing business environment know how important it is to find ways to increase efficiency and productivity. Still, new methods and different ways of thinking about work can be daunting, if not threatening. Managers who embrace the third work-life principle, however, see experimenting with work processes as an exciting opportunity to improve the organization's performance and the lives of its people at the same time. They have discovered that conflicts between work and personal priorities can actually be catalysts for identifying work inefficiencies that might otherwise have remained hidden or intractable. That's because taking a new set of parameters into account can allow people to question ways of doing business so ingrained that no one would think to consider changing them otherwise.

These managers encourage employees to question basic assumptions, such as the common sales mantra: "Real commitment means total availability." "Does it really?" they ask. "Can we find creative ways to demonstrate total commitment to our customers without being available every waking moment?" They also encourage employees to learn, through trial and error, about new ways to organize work that might well challenge the legitimacy of existing practices.

Many work practices are legacies of outdated industrial models in which employees had to be physically present during "normal" business hours. The managers who strike a work-life balance with their employees, however, recognize that newer telecommunication tools—such as e-mail, voice mail, teleconferencing, and computer networks—can create greater flexibility in how, when, where, and with whom work is accomplished. In addition, they are willing to explore alternative arrangements like job sharing to see if they can improve organizational efficiency while freeing up employees' time.

Hallie is a manager who—by meeting both business demands and her employees' personal needs—was able to reinvent the way work was done in her organization. As the new department director at a food services company, Hallie learned that she had inherited an older employee named Sarah, an administrative assistant who was perceived to be unmotivated and cynical. Her attitude, Hallie was told by other employees, badly hurt morale. They recommended, in fact, that she fire Sarah if she could.

At Hallie's first meeting with Sarah, she learned that Sarah enjoyed working with numbers but was not permitted to do finance work because of her inexperience with computers. Hallie also learned that Sarah was caring for her mother, who was in the late stages of a terminal illness. As her mother's condition deteriorated, Sarah found she had to go to her home in the morning and again at lunch to tend to her mother's physical and household needs. In addition, Sarah also managed her own home—chores, yard work, and paying the bills.

Hallie could have heard Sarah's story and asked, "How can I rid myself of this burden?" Instead she asked, "How can we work differently, in a way that will improve the department's performance and preserve the dignity of the employee?"

Together, Hallie and Sarah explored possible answers. They were able to identify inefficiencies in the department's work processes, including those in Sarah's job. The department had been formed recently as a result of the consolidation of several different groups. Yet Sarah was maintaining separate budgeting and inventory control systems. Combining them would streamline data collection and analysis.

Knowing of Sarah's interest in finance, Hallie arranged for her to be trained on Excel, on a new Excel-based budgetary system, and in basic analytical processes, which gave her greater control over the department's finances. The change had immediate effects.

Valuing productivity over face time is a necessary element in experimenting with work processes. Sarah now gathered more relevant data in a streamlined and logical manner, allowing managers to interpret the information faster and more intelligently. At the same time, working with numbers greatly increased Sarah's interest in her job. Her morale and performance improved markedly. And working on a computer made it easier for her to care for her mother; she could even work from home when her mother needed more attention. As a result of the change in the content and flexibility of her job, Sarah had an easier time coping with her mother's final days.

A Mutually Reinforcing System

Each of the three work-life principles might be practiced by itself, but more often they are practiced together. That's because the principles reinforce one another and, in fact, overlap to some degree. Encouraging employees to be explicit about their personal priorities, for instance, is a necessary element in recognizing and supporting an employee as a whole person. Valuing productivity over face time is a necessary element in experimenting with work processes. Both involve a manager caring more about the ends than the means. Let's look more, then, at all three principles working together.

Consider first the case of Sam, the director of a 24-hour command center at a pharmaceutical company's largest site, a plant with 8,000 employees. The 30-person center monitors more than 10,000 "hot spots" at the site, such as fire alarms; sewage lift stations; and, in particular, a hazardous manufacturing process. For example, the command center oversees several vaults that house chemicals being stored at minus 70 degrees Fahrenheit. Employees working in the vaults must wear special protective suits and are allowed to stay for only ten minutes at a time; if they stay longer, the center considers it an emergency and responds in kind. Such incidents are not uncommon and, as you might expect, work in the command center can be stressful.

Because the command center needed to be staffed around the clock, its schedule was always a challenge. Sam frequently had trouble filling the midnight to 8 A.M.

slots in particular. Shifts changed 21 times each week, and exchanging information between members of incoming and outgoing shifts was cumbersome. To make matters worse, the command center was about to be handed more work. The number of hot spots under its supervision was set to increase by 50% to 15,000 within the next year and perhaps even to double to 20,000 within two years.

Sam could have seen the burgeoning workload at the command center purely as a business problem and sought an exclusively business solution. How could he fill the center's schedule, keep overtime down, and make sure information was exchanged efficiently? But Sam also realized that a heavier workload was bound to have an impact on his staff's personal lives. Financial constraints made hiring more people out of the question. The existing staff would need to work longer hours under more stressful conditions. If he ignored those facts, Sam believed, any solution he arrived at would not be sustainable. The members of his staff were not robots but whole people with rich and varied lives. Just as the business imperatives had to be accounted for, so did his people's personal needs and concerns.

Sam's first step was to call his staff together and explicitly define the command center's business goals. He talked about how the group's work was essential for the safe operation of the entire site, including the critical research and manufacturing processes. He was open about how the center's workload was sure to increase and about the fact that they could not just throw more people at the problem.

Sam had a vision of the command center as more customer focused, proactively anticipating the needs of the site. He described to the group, for example, the need to improve the way manufacturing lines were shut down for maintenance and repair. He stressed the importance of forecasting needs as far in advance as possible, rather than waiting for an emergency to galvanize everyone to action. Sam knew that to achieve his vision, everyone would have to pay more attention to feedback from the center's customers, that the staff would need more training, and that there would simply be more plain, hard work—and he told them so. At the same time, he explicitly acknowledged that the demanding workload might have a negative impact on his employees' personal lives, and he invited them to describe to him and to one another how the schedule could adversely affect them.

After that discussion, Sam opened the door for radical experimentation with the way the command center was run. He asked the staff itself to design a solution to the scheduling problem that met not only the business needs he had outlined but also their own personal requirements. As many executives who operate according to the three principles do, Sam told the employees that no solution was out of bounds as long as it produced the results they were looking for. He also told them that they did not have to solve all the center's problems at once. They could test possible plans of action, gradually learning from those experiences what would work and what would not.

Within several weeks, Sam's people had developed a comprehensive new approach to staffing the center. They would work 12-hour shifts, three days on and four days off one week, four days on and three days off the next week. Over the course of two weeks, they would work 84 hours, which worked out to four more than they had in the past. But at the same time, work schedules would be steady and predictable, and their time off more concentrated. It added up to an acceptable trade-off.

The system has now been in place for more than two years, and it has far exceeded expectations. At work, the new schedule has eliminated seven shifts, which means that information is now exchanged seven fewer times, reducing errors and oversights during shift transfers. The predictability of the schedule has reduced overtime considerably, as well as the number of personal days the employees take. In addition, the new schedule has led to a better way to train supervisors. In the past, they had been stuck in the command center whenever there was an unexpected hole in the schedule. Often they were alone on the night shift, during which they learned little and potentially compromised safety. But now they are rotated systematically into the command center in all shifts to learn the processes, systems, and safety procedures.

Much to Sam's delight, the new system has allowed the center to become the proactive, customer-focused group he had envisioned. Now that staff members work on a set schedule and aren't scrambling to fill empty spots, they can spend more time on coordination and process improvements. For example, there was a time when sales of a new drug boomed, exceeding forecasts by 300%. Unfortunately, the drug's manufacturing line was scheduled to be closed for six days of maintenance. Working with production and maintenance supervisors, the command center was able to reduce shutdown time to two days.

Finally, because the schedule has become predictable and acceptable to all, there's less strife among employees and less strife between employees and management. In short, morale is up and stress is down. Not surprisingly, productivity has improved.

At home, the new schedule has allowed employees to meet their personal needs in ways that were not possible under the old system. One person was able finally to go to school during the day to earn a master's degree. Another earned a certificate degree on her days off. Many employees have told Sam that simply feeling that their lives are predictable has allowed them to relax when they are home and plan more personal projects and events. The new schedule has been so successful from a lifestyle point of view that, somewhat ironically, it has created a high demand to work in the command center. "We are a magnet now for transfers and new hires," Sam recently observed.

We found another example of the three principles working in tandem at a global, 80,000-employee manufacturing company where senior executives were anxious to determine the best way to transfer knowledge from region to region. They decided to test a radical new approach that had two parts: a computer-based data warehouse that would allow sales representatives to collect and share sales and marketing information in real time and a territory management system that would allow each sales rep to run a fully functioning, independent operation. The success or failure of the two pilot projects would determine the company's direction for global marketing and sales.

A task force consisting of three men and three women was created to oversee and coordinate the pilot projects. It was headed by one of the women, Terry. From the outset, pressure on the group was intense; the company's leaders believed that the way the organization managed the process of learning and of transferring information was critical to its competitive success. Despite the pressure for results, Terry strongly believed that if she let business objectives nullify personal ones, the task force would fail on all counts. "To ignore people's personal issues was unrealistic," she noted. At the time, all the team members had significant personal issues: two pregnancies, three recent births, one person on a part-time schedule, another in a demanding M.B.A. program at night, and still another in the midst of a family separation.

Before the task force's first meeting, Terry met individually with each member to discuss the demands he or she faced in the coming year and to help identify each person's spectrum of priorities. Then, at the first group meeting, Terry led a discussion of business objectives. She explicitly defined what the company's leaders expected of the team, as well as the timetables and specific tasks involved. She identified how the team's performance would be measured and what kind of results would constitute success.

Next, Terry opened up the dialogue on personal priorities and brought in the discussion of roles. She asked a couple of questions to get it going: "Despite the amount of work we will all have to do, what personal priorities do you want to make sure are not compromised? In other words, what is most important for you from a personal perspective as we embark on this work?" Team members voluntarily disclosed challenges in their personal lives, which they felt comfortable doing because of their prior separate conversations with Terry. The meeting concluded with the team brainstorming about how business and personal objectives could be reached at the same time. Members decided, for instance, that they needed to know how to do one another's jobs so that they could cover if anyone had to miss work. They also decided that they needed to constantly keep abreast of everyone's schedules and personal demands so that no one would be taken by surprise, and the flow of work would not be disrupted, if a member was absent.

As the pilots progressed, weekly planning meetings continued to focus on both business and personal priorities. Members did learn one another's jobs inside and out, and constantly updated everyone on the demands of their personal lives. As one team member said, "We knew each other's home routines, school holidays, and soccer practice schedules. It was easy to do this because we talked about everything up front." The lengthy stretch needed for a christening in Paris or for a six-week vacation that had been booked a year in advance—and other personal time constraints—were known and accounted for as legitimate business issues.

As the pilots concluded, there could be no doubt that the team's results were impressive. All of their ambitious deadlines were met or beaten. Moreover, the fact that everyone knew everyone else's job added to the creativity and value of the team's output. Most important, the team achieved its goal of developing systems for knowledge transfer that could be used throughout the company worldwide.

The three principles are typically put in practice by managers "flying under the radar" of officially sanctioned programs.

They were evaluated in a 360-degree process by their customers, team members, and their senior management sponsors. The project was successful from every business measure they had established.

Not surprisingly, the team members' lives and careers were enhanced by their experience on the task force. No one had to compromise personal priorities because of work. And, as one team member said, because of the openness and trust created within the team, "the project was the most satisfying work environment I have ever been in." Professionally, members of the team flourished after the project was completed. Terry, for instance, received a major promotion and now heads up the strategic-support function for one of the company's largest regions.

Getting Beyond the Status Quo

As we've said, the three principles are typically put into practice by managers "flying under the radar." Our next case, however, involves the manager of an HR department at a prominent accounting firm who actually used the principles to put the issues on the radar screen, thereby enhancing the performance of his organization's business-assurance department and the life of one of its senior associates, an aspiring novelist we'll call Jane.

Jane had joined the firm after graduating from college with a double major in accounting and English. She enjoyed her work—and was considered a strong performer by her superiors—but she also yearned to find time for her real passion, creative writing. After rummaging through the materials that were handed out back at her orientation, Jane came across a pamphlet that discussed the company's policy on alternative work schedules. She had hoped there would be a way to develop a schedule that would take advantage of the seasonal nature of the accounting business and allow her to carve out significant blocks of time for writing. But none of the examples of alternative schedules in the pamphlet came close to meeting her needs. Even though it felt risky to ask for something radically different, Jane approached Harry, the HR manager responsible for her department. In a way, there was no one else to turn to. Because of the project-based nature of Jane's work, the managers supervising her job were always changing. Much to her surprise, Harry was receptive and said he would be glad to work with Jane to craft a solution to her work-life dilemma.

Jane began by suggesting she reduce her workload from 12 to 8 clients. The change would mean that in the off-season she'd have sufficient chunks of time to focus on writing. Client by client, Harry and Jane decided which ones to keep and which to pass on to other associates. They then charted out the expected work for the upcoming year, making sure there would be enough time both for fulfilling her clients' needs and for writing.

At first, the plan seemed like a good one. Unfortunately, Jane quickly began to doubt how realistic it was. Often during her writing time, she would get a call from the central assignments department, putting her on another job. Although Jane knew she could legitimately decline those assignments because she had already completed the work she had contracted for, she was concerned that refusing work might have ramifications for her career later on. Hesitantly, she approached Harry a second time.

Harry was again receptive, inviting Gabriel, a member of the central assignments department, to join the discussions. The three of them then developed a method by which Jane's hours were logged so that there no longer would be any confusion about when she had extra time available for work and when the extra time was reserved for writing. Jane also suggested that she change the way she did her work. Could she try e-mailing and faxing her clients, she asked, instead of assuming that a face-to-face meeting was always necessary? Harry agreed to let her experiment.

The benefits of the new arrangement became apparent within the year, particularly with regard to Jane's capacity to contribute to the firm. With fewer clients, Jane felt more focused at work and thus more committed and effective. Previously, she had been moved from project to project and sometimes from crisis to crisis. Now she could plan her time in advance and concentrate on end results more creatively. In fact, she found that for the first time she had enough energy and time to reflect on better ways to get her projects done. Her clients responded positively; Jane's efficiency allowed her to work more quickly, which in some cases reduced their fees. And meanwhile, Jane was able to write two novels.

Three years later, still following this alternative work schedule, Jane was promoted to manager at the same time as others in her cohort. As a manager herself, Jane now practices the three principles. She believes they help her keep and motivate quality employees. Not only is it costly to replace a good employee, but, she notes, "people who are constantly under pressure will take the path of least resistance, doing things the way it was done last year instead of looking for ways to improve on the product." Furthermore, Jane points out that, unlike in other work groups at the company, "my group doesn't have to work weekends. Instead, we've found out everyone's parameters, discussed what work needs to get done, and focused on the end results."

Recently, Harry and Jane served together on a task force that's looking for ways to apply more broadly what they learned from practicing the three principles. They are exploring the development of a project database that would make it easier to anticipate the workload in advance and even out the assignments among the associates. They are looking into the possibility of defining expected work hours more explicitly. They believe that this will encourage a new attitude whereby excessive work hours will be seen not as a measure of commitment but as an indication of the need for better planning.

Although Jane and Harry are plainly aware of the benefits to the business of the approach they've developed, Jane is also absolutely clear about the personal benefits. "Neither activity, work nor writing, was appealing in isolation. I didn't want to be a starving writer, forced to write to earn a living. But I also felt that if I stopped practicing my writing, my creative side would die, and then the job would just become a job. Until we worked out this solution, I felt like it had to be an either-or choice, but now I see it doesn't have to be that way. Both sides can win."

A New Breed of Managers

If the three principles are so effective, why aren't they more widespread? There is no single answer. Some managers block the new approach to balancing work and life because they are bound by tradition and continue to value face time for its own sake. They believe that productivity is a function of time spent in the office—not energy invested in the work. Other managers are simply unaware that their employees might be able to bring skills and knowledge to their jobs from their lives beyond work. And still other managers consider the whole topic of striking a balance between work and personal life as a women's issue—in other words, not their problem.

We have also found that managers resist the three principles because they fear that taking an employee's personal priorities into account will create either a sense of entitlement or feelings of resentment. Take the case of Sarah and Hallie again. Once Hallie allowed Sarah to work at home to care for her ailing mother, these managers might reason, what's to stop everyone in the office from asking for some sort of special treatment to make his or her life more convenient or enjoyable? If we oblige, these managers might argue, we risk creating a slippery-slope situation in which the organization is expected to strike a work-life balance for every employee. If we don't, we are certain to anger people who feel slighted. Why should Sarah be allowed to work at home, another employee may ask, if I still have to come into the office when my child or husband is sick? What makes her more deserving than me?

It's understandable that managers worry about setting off waves of entitlement and/or resentment. But interestingly, the managers in our research who use the three principles rarely run into that. Because these managers deal with all of their people individually, every one of their employees does, in fact, receive "special" treatment in terms of a work plan that takes personal priorities into account. Therefore, there is less chance for resentment to fester. As for entitlement, the enormous loyalty these employees feel toward their managers usually outweighs it. Indeed, when a manager helps his or her employees strike a work-life balance, they feel grateful more than anything else.

In reality, following the three principles does not involve that much more time and energy than managing in more traditional ways.

Even when managers are inclined to operate with the three principles, many tell us that they don't because they believe it would be impractical and complicated. How time consuming it must be to delve into the varied priorities and life roles of every employee, they argue. And imagine how much energy it would take to create a series of individual action plans that fulfill both professional and personal goals.

But we have found that, in reality, following the three principles does not involve that much more time or energy than managing in more traditional ways. Virtually all managers today are held accountable for developing their employees professionally—that is, they already engage in discussions about what their people want and need from work and what they are expected to contribute. To bring personal-life priorities and goals into the conversation really only involves asking two or three more questions. And often the answers to those questions are so illuminating, they make the development process more honest—and more efficient.

Sometimes the "work" of the three principles can be delegated to the employees themselves, who can apply them personally and to their dealings with one another. In fact, we have seen that people become quickly engaged in this process as they come to realize that the solutions they develop will benefit both the business and their own lives. Consequently, the principles need not sap any more time or energy than conducting management as usual.

Out from Under the Radar

No two companies—indeed, no two managers— approach the relationship between work and personal life exactly the same way. But it is fair to say that all organizational practices fall along a continuum. On one end is the *trade-off* approach, whereby either the business wins or personal life wins, but not both. Further along is the *integrated* approach, in which employee and manager work together to find ways to meet both the company's and the employee's needs. That approach is indeed becoming more common, as an increasing number of companies use "life friendly" policies to attract and retain talented people.

Taken together, the three principles fall at the far end of the continuum—the *leveraged* approach, in which the practices used to strike a work-life balance actually add value to the business. Not only do the three principles seem to help people live more satisfying personal lives, but they also help identify inefficiencies in work processes and illuminate better ways to get work done. Think of the pharmaceutical company's command center, for example. Using the three principles, its staff created a new and successful solution to its managerial problems that neither the trade-off nor the integrated approach could have achieved.

The growing cadre of managers who use the three principles to help their employees strike a work-life balance typically do so without official sanction. But perhaps as the business impact of their approach becomes better known and understood, a shift will occur. Managers who once flew below the radar will themselves become beacons of change.

Where to Begin

PUTTING THE THREE PRINCIPLES into practice does not happen overnight. It can't—the changes required by this new approach are too substantial to be instituted without stops and starts, and periods of evaluation. Therefore, when managers ask us how to get started, we often suggest that they begin by applying the principles to one employee. Think of Steve, the senior executive who once expected his staff to work from 7 A.M. to 10 P.M. He used the three principles to help one person—Jim—strike a meaningful balance between work and personal life. The arrangement—and its successful impact on both Jim and the business—gave Steve the experience and the confidence he needed to apply the three principles more broadly. Eventually, the principles became the foundation of his management style.

A second way to get started with the principles is to initiate an organizational dialogue about integrating work and personal life goals. In small-team settings, a manager might even lead the process of creating a work-life philosophy statement. We have seen such dialogues facilitate the implementation of the principles by bringing to light thorny issues such as the organization's level of commitment to striking a work-life balance or employees' fears about sharing private information about their personal priorities and life roles.

As a third starting point, we suggest that managers try applying the three principles to themselves to find out how well they personally have leveraged work and personal life. First, a manager might ask, "How well do I clarify my own life goals? Do I know where work falls in my list of priorities? What trade-offs am I willing to make to achieve my goals?"

Second, a manager might consider, "Do I understand my varied life roles—such as parent, child, cub scout master—in terms of how they overlap and when they must be kept separate? That is, have I considered what skills and knowledge can be transferred from one role to another, and have I explicitly formulated the boundaries of each role?" Some executives, for instance, will not check voice mail on weekends; others let their work and personal lives blend.

And finally, a manager can explore his or her comfort level with the third principle of continual experimentation by asking, "Do I regularly challenge the way I myself approach tasks, both at work and at home? How do I react when other people suggest new ways to get things done? Am I defensive or intrigued?"

A self-assessment is useful because it shows managers who want to embark on the journey of striking a balance between work and personal life how sensitive they may or may not be to the struggles of employees trying to do the same. Does that mean people who don't have their own house in order should avoid managing with the principles? Not necessarily, but they should be aware that striking a work-life balance, like many other aspects of effective management, can take time, energy, and commitment. Given its added value, however, the process appears to be well worth the investment.

Originally published in November–December 1998
Reprint 98605

Must Success Cost So Much?

PAUL A. LEE EVANS

Executive Summary

UNDENIABLY, MANY PEOPLE who reach executive levels in organizations do so at the expense of their personal lives. They spend long hours at difficult and tension-filled jobs and retreat to their homes not for comfort and sustenance but for a place to hide or to vent feelings left over from a bad day at the office. Yet other executives who endure the same long hours and tension-filled jobs come home full of energy and excited by the day. What distinguishes the two groups of people? After studying more than 2,000 executives and interviewing many husbands and wives, these authors have found that, psychological differences aside, the executives who successfully cross the line from job to private life are able to do three things better than the other executives. They adapt well to change in jobs, they find the right jobs for them, and they handle career disappointments well. The authors

31

discuss these sources of potential negative emotional spillover; then they investigate how organizations might minimize obstacles to coordinating one's private and professional lives.

A GOOD NUMBER OF EXECUTIVES accept the cliché that success always demands a price and that the price is usually deterioration of private life. This cliché does not always reflect reality, however—some executives seem to be exempt. What distinguishes the executives who pay a heavy personal price for their success from those who are able to maintain and develop fulfilling private lives?

In studying the private and professional lives of more than 2,000 managers for nearly five years, we've seen that some very successful executives have meaningful private lives. One thing that does not distinguish these executives is professional commitment. (To succeed, individuals have to give their jobs a high priority in their lives.) Nor is it easier for these executives to develop a private life. For everyone, it is difficult.

What *does* distinguish the two groups is this: the executives whose private lives deteriorate are subject to the negative effects of what we call emotional spillover; work consistently produces negative feelings that overflow into private life. In contrast, the other group of executives have learned to manage their work and careers so that negative emotional spillover is minimized, and thus they achieve a balance between their professional and private lives.

After countless exchanges with managers and their wives and after careful analysis of research data, we concluded that the major determinant of work's impact on private life is whether negative emotional feelings aroused at work spill over into family and leisure time. When an executive experiences worry, tension, fear, doubt, or stress intensely, he is not able to shake these feelings when he goes home, and they render him psychologically unavailable for a rich private life. The manager who is unhappy in his work has a limited chance of being happy at home—no matter how little he travels, how much time he spends at home, or how frequently he takes a vacation.

When individuals feel competent and satisfied in their work—not simply contented, but challenged in the right measure by what they are doing—negative spillover does not exist. During these periods executives are open to involvement in private life; they experience positive spillover. When work goes well, it can have the same effect as healthy physical exercise—instead of leading to fatigue, it is invigorating.

If things go right at work, a feeling of well-being places people in the right mood to relate to others. They open up, they are available, they may search for contact. That, of course, does not guarantee that such contact will be successful. A person may not be skillful at it, or there may be deep conflicts from the past that make contact difficult. But when the executive feels good at work, contact at home is at least possible.

We can summarize our findings this way: for an ambitious person, a well-functioning professional life is a necessary though not sufficient condition for a well-functioning private one.

For the time being, our study has focused on male managers only. We have not yet studied female executives, but our exchanges with some women and our reading of the literature on women managers lead us to believe strongly that the ideas we present apply to them as well.

The dilemmas and conflicts women face in trying to manage the relationship between their professional and private lives may be even more difficult than those faced by men. While in many cultures it is acceptable for men to specialize in their professional roles and delegate the main responsibility for private life to their wives, our impression is that even in the more liberal and advanced cultures the married woman who chooses to pursue a career is still expected to be responsible for the quality of the couple's private life.

Women are under more pressure to manage skillfully the boundaries between professional and private life. They are probably more aware of what causes the conflicts than many men. As increasing numbers of women join the work force, these issues are being more openly considered at work.

The Price Some Managers Pay

Even though we recognize that positive spillover exists, for the most part in this article we're going to be concerned with the negative emotions that spill over from work into executives' private lives. What are its sources? How can individuals manage it, and what can companies do to minimize the likelihood that people will suffer from it?

The experience of this 36-year-old manager typifies the spillover phenomenon: "When I started working for my boss four years ago, that affected my family life. He was very different from my previous boss. He was a bit of a tyrant. From working with someone who was terri-

bly easygoing to someone who's an absolute dynamo—
that certainly had an influence on my family life. It
made me slightly—how can I put it? Well, I'd come
home to my wife talking about him, about decisions he
had reversed on a certain proposal I'd made. I'd talk it
over with my wife, but I couldn't get it out of my mind,
because it was such a different way of operating from
my previous boss."

All of us have experienced spillover at one time or
another in our careers. The problem is that some executives lead lifestyles that pave the way for never-ending
spillover. Such an executive's wife is likely to react with
this sort of comment: "What annoys me is when he
comes home tense and exhausted. He flops into a chair
and turns on the TV. Or else he worries, and it drives me
up the wall."

Work spills over into private life in two ways: through
fatigue and through emotional tension, like worry.
Fatigue is the natural consequence of a hectic day at the
office. But curiously enough, a hectic day—if it has gone
well—can make us feel less worn out, often almost ener-
getic. On the other hand, a boring day at the office, when
the executive feels he has not accomplished anything, is
exhausting. He comes home tired. Home is not a place
for private life; it simply becomes a haven—a place to
rest, relax, and recharge batteries to survive the next day.

Worrying, the other symptom of negative emotional
spillover, is caused by frustration, self-doubt, and unfinished business. One wife puts it this way: "Yes, his mind
is often on other things. Yes, he often worries and it *does*
disturb the family life. When he is like that he can't stand
the noise of the children. . . . He can't stand the fact
that the children are tired. In general we have dinner
together so that he can be with them. And obviously they

chatter, they spill things, they tease each other—and he blows his top. He is tense and uptight—it's disturbing; I can't stand it. I have to try to mediate between them and cool things down. The only thing is to finish everything as soon as possible and get everyone quickly off to bed."

The feelings that spill over from work are acted out at home. Sometimes they are expressed through psychological absence, sometimes through acts of aggression. One loses one's temper with the children. One explodes in fury if one's wife makes a minor mistake. Such aggression is visible and painful, but withdrawal is equally damaging to family relationships. As one wife said:

"My husband is not one of those men who vents all his frustrations on the family. One cannot reproach him for being aggressive or for beating his wife. Instead he closes up like a shell. Total closure. The time he thinks he spends here isn't spent here."

Because psychological withdrawal can make a person blind to what is going on at home, it can have very serious consequences. A 40-year-old executive described the most painful period of his marriage this way:

"It was just after the birth of the third child, eight years ago. The birth coincided with a move to another part of the country and with a complete change in job. And there I have to admit that I was completely unaware of the consequences that all this had for my wife. She was overloaded with work and worries. It went on for some time, and I just wasn't aware of what was happening. Finally she fell ill and had to be hospitalized. It was only then that it began to dawn on me. I was quite unconscious of everything I was doing."

"You were overloaded in your work?"

"Yes. Well, not really overloaded. I was worried about my work. I didn't feel very sure of myself and so was very worried. . . . It was the time of a merger between two companies and a period of great uncertainty. That had led to my new job and the move. And I just couldn't get my work out of my mind. I think back even today—the uncertainties of the time were real. It was normal, but anyway I couldn't get the work out of my mind. Today I'm much more sure of myself. I find it a lot easier to switch off."

When negative emotions spill over, managers often express dissatisfaction with their lifestyles and complain of wanting more time for private life. But because their minds are numbed by tension, these people cannot use even their available time in a fulfilling way. Some report needing a double martini just to summon the energy to switch on the television. Many read the newspaper, not because they're interested in world events, but to escape into personal privacy. Some mooch around in the basement or the garden as a way of just getting through the day.

Again and again, the wives of these executives express the same idea: "I don't really mind the amount of work he has to do. That is, if he is happy in his work. What I resent is the unhappiness that he brings home."

Or sometimes they agree with this 42-year-old wife: "The very best moment in our marriage is, without any doubt, right now. We have never before had such a complete life together. The children are interesting to my husband and he is very happy with his work. On the other hand, the most difficult moments have been when he wasn't happy with what he was doing."

MANAGING SPILLOVER

To have a healthy private life, one must manage the negative emotions that arise at work. When we began our investigation into the work lives and private lives of managers five years ago, we held the biased belief that these two sides of life are in fundamental conflict with each other. During these five years we have gathered more and more evidence suggesting that, among managers at least, individual and organizational interests can be in harmony. Moreover, a healthy professional life is a precondition for a healthy private one.

Job and home can be in harmony and mutually reinforce each other if—and only if—one avoids various pitfalls in the management of self and career and one copes satisfactorily with the emotions that arise at work. Conversely, executives who fail to manage the emotional side of work achieve professional success at the expense of private life.

Let's look now at what the executive can do to manage the emotional side of work better. We single out three major causes of negative emotional spillover: the problems of adapting to a new job, the lack of fit between a person and his job, and career disappointments.

Coping with a New Job

Without doubt, the most common trigger of spillover tension is the process of settling into a new job following promotion, reorganization, or a move to another company. Since all of us change jobs from time to time, we all experience spillover caused by the problems of adaptation. Having to familiarize ourselves with a new task, learn to work with new people, settle in a different town and environment, and establish new relationships with superiors, subordinates, and peers—all at the same time—overloads our emotional systems.

That work dominates the emotional life of a person adapting to a new job is natural and necessary. It allows him to master major changes. Once that is done, the spillover effects begin to fade away.

What is vital is that the individual assess and recognize how important a change he (and his family) face when he changes jobs. The more new skills the job requires and the more radical the change in environment, the longer the adaptation period is likely to be and the longer the negative spillover is likely to last. To deny this reality in an attempt to persuade a reluctant family that the job change will also be good for them is risky.

Top managers often fail to assess correctly the magnitude of the changes and adaptations they ask of executives and their families. Often individual executives, driven by their own ambition, also fail to assess accurately the difficulty of tasks they accept. Only a realistic evaluation of the degree of change executives and their families will face allows them to come through the process of adaptation relatively unscathed.

In talking to executive couples, we have found too often the case of the ambitious executive who accepted an exciting job in a developing country that sounded like a wonderful opportunity and a major career step. His wife was unhappy about it, but there was no heart-to-heart discussion about the decision. The wife felt that her husband's mind was made up and was reluctant to hold him back. Her fears were half-assuaged by his assurances that the move would be challenging and exciting and that he would be there to help out. They moved.

What executives do not realize is that the change to a new and important job, to a new locale, and to a new culture will create massive amounts of tension. The negative spillover into private life will be immense. For a year or more, they will have minimal psychological availability for private life. If their wives expect and need that availability, its absence will aggravate the adaptation problems that they are undergoing themselves. Far too often, the story ends catastrophically for all concerned. And yet it doesn't need to happen this way. We have heard executives describe enthusiastically how similar moves brought their families together and how dealing with the difficulties of adaptation as a family was a most positive experience.

What accounts for the difference in experiences? These latter executives analyzed the change carefully with their families before the move, negotiated the decision with them, openly expressed the problems they would all confront, and did not promise what they could not deliver.

Most wives will understand and accept that for some time their husbands will be preoccupied with the job and won't be readily available. If they recognize this in advance and as long as they know that emotional spillover will fade away, they may even support him at this difficult time. But sometimes spillover does not fade away. The new job turns out to be beyond the person's talents or capacities.

If after a reasonable period of time—say, one year— negative spillover is increasing rather than fading away, a misfit situation (where the only way of mastering the job is through sheer brute energy rather than skill) could be in the making. Because wives experience the spillover consequences directly, they are good judges as to whether it is increasing or decreasing. If it's increasing, the time has come to negotiate a move out.

Taking the Right Job

The lack of fit between an individual and a job is the second most common source of negative spillover. Judgments on the "shape" of people and jobs are difficult to make; square pegs are often put in round holes. Top managers may overemphasize skills and experience while ignoring the very important factors of personality and individual goals. Consider the experiences of Jack and Melinda.

Three years ago, Jack was a computer company's research manager, content in his job and very ambitious. Top management offered him a promotion to a job as manager of administrative services. While at first Jack didn't like the position offered him, management persuaded him to accept it by arguing that it would be an important step in his career development. Since Jack's ambition was to become research director, the argument seemed logical. The new job would give him administrative experience that would help qualify him for the post he wanted. Jack accepted the job.

Jack has already spent three years in this job, yet spillover tension is not on the wane. On the contrary, during the past three years it has increased steadily and is now an almost inextricable part of his life. But while he is hurting, his wife Melinda and his two children are hurting even more.

Melinda talks of how Jack has brought nothing but sadness and tension into the family's life since he undertook his new job. Since then, she says, "He hasn't even been interested in talking about our problems." In fact, she has often considered divorce.

For his part, Jack finds it difficult to say anything positive about his job. "You meet interesting people and a wide variety of situations," he says, "but one part of the work consists of acting as the office boy to deal with everyone's banal problems." The other part consists of negotiating with trade union officials on grievances, a duty that Jack finds tiring and frustrating. "You have no authority over anyone," he says, "and what I didn't realize at the beginning is that one doesn't have any real contact with the people in research."

The tension and doubt that Jack feels—and which his wife experiences even more strongly—are growing. At the end of a two-hour interview, he spoke of the feeling of being trapped: "I'm not really content in this job, but if I do well it will help me in my next job in research. It's a thankless task, being at everybody's beck and call. The trouble is that it's getting to me. I can't take the strain much longer. I went to my boss last month and told him that I want to move back to research. He told me that they would take care of that in due time, that I was doing a grand job now, and that they needed me here.

"The trouble is—did he really mean it that I was doing a grand job? I feel that things can only go downhill from here. And I'm drifting further and further away from research."

LACK OF FIT

Jack is a misfit. However valid or invalid his reasons for accepting his present job, the work does not suit his personality. It makes him permanently tense without satisfying him. Yet because he took the job as a "stepping stone," he *must* perform.

Lacking deep interest and natural skill for the work, the misfit can only compensate with an over investment of energy. This investment may lead to success—but at the price of enormous internal tension, reinforced fear of failure, and the suspension of an investment in private life.

Tension and deep fear of failure are the natural consequences of going against one's grain. People who take jobs for which they are ill-fitted are often afraid that their weaknesses will show, that they will be found out. These inner doubts can be so intense that no amount of external recognition or acknowledgment of success can eliminate them.

For misfits the ultimate irony is that, instead of decreasing with each new success, fear of failure increases. Outward success does not reassure them. Instead, their successes trap them in jobs they do not enjoy. With their bridges burned behind them, they feel snared in situations that create permanent and increasing tension.

Let us define what we mean by the fit between individual and job. A perfect fit occurs when you experience three positive feelings at the same time: you feel competent, you enjoy the work, and you feel that your work and your moral values coincide. To express this in another way, a job should fit not only with skills and abilities but also with motives and values.

A misfit situation occurs whenever one of these three conditions is absent. In the case of the *total misfit*, none of the conditions is fulfilled: he is not particularly competent at what he does, he enjoys few aspects of his work, and he feels ashamed doing things that go against his values or ideals. Jack, the manager we just described, is an example.

Absence of skill. The *competence misfit* enjoys his work and is proud of what he does. He works hard enough to keep his job, but he is not sure of his ability to really master the work. For example, a manager in a line position may find it difficult to make decisions, or someone taking a personnel administrator's job hoping to broaden his skills may not work well with people. For the time being, those executives may manage well, but they live with the persistent fear that things will get out of hand. This sense of insecurity tends to diminish their enjoyment of the job and spills over into their private lives.

This "competence misfit" most typically happens to people in the early stages of their careers, when they haven't yet found out what they are good at doing. It is the type of misfit that organizations are most sensitive to, which they try hardest to avoid. But two other kinds of misfit, which most organizations fail to recognize, are equally important. We call them the "enjoyment misfit" and the "moral misfit."

Dislike for the job. An *enjoyment misfit* occurs when an individual is competent at his job and proud of doing it but does not like it. One executive had the necessary qualities to be a manager and was promoted to a managerial job even though he would have rather remained in a technical position. Despite his preference for individual challenge over the laborious process of working through other people, he succumbed to a sense of duty and to unanimous pressure and accepted the job. He is unhappy in his new job and consequently suffers from negative spillover.

The most frequent cause of "enjoyment misfit" is intrinsic dislike of various work characteristics, but other causes are common as well. Staying in a job for too long can transform enjoyment into boredom; persons can be competent but see what they do as predictable variations of a humdrum theme. Having too much work to do can also destroy enjoyment: some people, finding it very difficult to say no to challenges and tasks they enjoy doing, agree to do too much. The consequent stress gradually erodes the intrinsic pleasure of the tasks.

Different values. The last type of misfit, *moral* misfit, results when individuals enjoy their work and are competent but do not feel proud of what they do, when they feel they compromise their values. A sales manager we met, for example, was good at his job, but he did not believe in the merits of the product he was selling. He would not have bought it himself and could not wholeheartedly recommend it to others. He used to reassure himself by saying that "as long as there is a market for it, it must be O.K." After a successful and important sale, rather than feeling proud of himself he would come out feeling "thank goodness that's over."

The negative spillover created by going along with unethical business practices (such as bribing foreign officials) has two additional painful twists to it. The person fears potential legal consequences, and he cannot vent his feelings by expressing them to others because the position dictates secrecy.

Each of these ways of not fitting a job is dangerous. If individuals accept tasks for which they lack the competence, they risk feeling continual self-doubt. If they accept jobs for which they are skilled but which they do not like doing, they will be bored. If they accept jobs in which they do not feel pride, they will not feel at peace with themselves.

The incompetent misfit may be the only type of misfit the organization is able to spot; whatever the cause of the misfit, however, the individuals and their families will suffer. For an individual in top management to avoid putting the wrong person in the wrong job, it is essential to understand what causes some of the mistakes.

WHY PEOPLE TAKE THE WRONG JOB

We find four main reasons why people are in the wrong jobs: the strong attraction of external rewards, organizational pressure, inability to say no, and lack of self-knowledge or self-assessment. Let's examine each one of these issues in turn.

External rewards. We all like and need money and have some healthy needs for status and recognition as well. But because in our Western society having these things implies that one is a "good" person, we sometimes put too much value on them. As a result, many people end up doing what will bring rewards rather than what fits them. They are seen as good members of society but don't feel good about themselves.

Executives we spoke with often justified accepting jobs they didn't really want on the ground that the material rewards the jobs provided were essential to realizing a fulfilling private life. They fail to realize (except in hindsight) that no matter how much they earn, no matter how much status is attached to the position, their private lives will suffer through emotional spillover if the job doesn't fit them.

Organizational pressures. When management approaches an individual in the organization or outside it to offer him a job, in most cases it does so after carefully analyzing available candidates. The person chosen is usually the one management deems most competent for the job.

But management pays little if any attention to the two other dimensions of fit—will the person enjoy the job and will he be proud of it? If it assesses these dimensions at all, management will often dismiss any problem as an individual or personal concern. A person's capacity to do the job well is all that counts. Some managers assume that if he does not feel he will like it or be proud of it, then he will say no; some also assume that if he doesn't say no, the personal issues don't exist.

But here is the problem. When management reaches its final decision and offers the person the promotion or the new job, he is no longer simply a candidate for that job. Management has made a statement that he is the best person available. To refuse is to deny management what it wants. Of course, he is free to say no on emotional grounds; but is he really? The pressures to accept are considerable.

Management often adopts a selling attitude that manifests itself in a variety of ways. The rewards and incentives are expressively described, the fact that this is a "unique opportunity" is stressed, and the argument that "this will be good for your career" is emphasized. If the individual points out that he may lack some of the necessary skills for the job, management is likely to say that this is "an exceptional opportunity to develop such skills," expressing vague doubts about the future otherwise. At the end of the process, management often brings the ultimate pressure to bear. It makes it clear that a decision has to be reached quickly, that an answer is expected "let's say, in 72 hours."

By this time many executives will have succumbed to the appeal of external rewards or to the fear of saying no or of showing hesitation. Nevertheless, the best of them will indeed insist on enough time to analyze as thoroughly as possible the intrinsic characteristics of the job and the extent to which it fits them.

These people are deeply aware that their decisions will influence not only every working hour in the years ahead but also every hour of their private lives. And these are the people most likely to avoid becoming misfits and suffering from massive spillover. In most cases, their attitudes are reinforced by a real concern for their families and a deep understanding of the impact that changing jobs may have on them.

Above all, such executives realize that they hold the main responsibility for managing their careers and are unwilling to transfer that responsibility to anybody else.

The ability to say no. If learning to ask for sufficient time to think over accepting a job is difficult, learning to say no is even more difficult, particularly in times of economic crisis.

Learning to say no requires, first of all, the ability to estimate realistically the consequences of refusal. Many people assume fearsome consequences that they often are too afraid to test. But one also has to estimate realistically the negative effects of acceptance. Executives we spoke to mentioned they had sometimes made the decision easier by minimizing the difficulties they would face.

Ability to assess consequences realistically is one of the characteristics of highly successful people. They can do this because they have the final and most important quality of people who want to avoid spillover—namely, self-knowledge and the ability to assess themselves accurately.

Self-assessment. Much of our behavior is rooted in unconscious motives, and it is difficult to know that part of ourselves. Also, as we age we are continually changing and acquiring new experiences. So, even under the best of circumstances, to assess whether one will fit with a new job is difficult.

Self-assessment implies that one can accurately recognize one's competences—acknowledging limitations as well as strengths, identifying what brings pleasure or pain, and knowing what elicits pride or guilt in different work situations. It requires admitting to feelings rather than masking them.

The raw data for self-assessment are past experiences. Because of limited experiences, the task is especially difficult for the younger manager. During one's 20s and early 30s, the only way to assess oneself is to take different jobs in different companies to find out what kind of work one does best, enjoys most, and finds most meaningful. Our research indicates that foreclosing this phase of exploration too quickly may have negative consequences later in one's career.[1]

This exploration, however, does not need to be a blind process. Under ideal circumstances, a mentor successfully guides the younger person in the trial and error stages of his career. The mentor—an older, experienced, and trusted guide (often a boss with whom one enjoys an open and special relationship)—does more than simply provide new challenges and experiences. This mentor also helps the younger manager learn from those experiences what his skills, needs, and values are, and thus speeds up the process of self-assessment.

No matter how well this process of starting one's own career and finding one's professional identity goes, the individual will suffer from considerable tension and stress. Managers at this stage in life are predominantly oriented toward launching their careers, and emotional spillover often pervades private life.

After such a period of exploration and with better knowledge of themselves, some individuals in their mid-30s eventually find jobs or positions that fit them in the three dimensions outlined earlier. The young man assessing a job asks himself above all "Can I do it?" But the more mature man asks two other questions as well: "Will I enjoy doing it?" and "Is it worth doing?" He is likely to accept the job only if all three answers are positive.

People at this stage in their careers turn more toward their private lives. They are no longer content simply with the competence fit. They aim for total fit that ensures minimal spillover and full availability for private life. They can achieve this if they have developed sufficient self-knowledge to guide their early careers, to become mentors themselves.[2]

For some people, self-knowledge grows with experience, and consequently they are able to manage their careers and avoid spillover. Others, however, fail to learn from experience and as a result are likely to suffer from the third main cause of spillover—namely, career disappointment.

Learning from Disappointments

Prevention is better than cure. Individuals skilled at self-assessment run a smaller risk not only of finding themselves in the wrong job but also of suffering serious disappointments. But all of us face disappointment at one time or another in our careers. It can have immense psychological impact, especially if work is an important part of our lives.

The most frequent type of disappointment that we have found in our research is experienced by the older manager whose career flattens out below the level he expected to reach. More or less consciously, he recognizes that he has plateaued. Individual signals of the end—a turned-down promotion, a merit raise refused, a bad appraisal, or a shuffling aside in a reorganization— are bitter blows. When deeply hurt, most of us will automatically react in a defensive way. While some individuals can eventually react healthily and learn from a painful experience, many become disillusioned and turn into bitter, plateaued performers. Often such executives disengage from activity. Abraham Zaleznik suggests that two things are necessary to cope well with disappointment: the ability "to become intimately acquainted with one's own emotional reactions" and the capacity to "face the disappointment squarely." And, he adds, "The temptation and the psychology of individual response to disappointment is to avoid the pain of self-examination. If an avoidance pattern sets in, the individual will pay dearly for it later."[3] In all cases, the danger is distortion of reality.

In our contacts with executives, we have found ample confirmation of Zaleznik's observations. It is indeed difficult for people to face disappointment squarely. The experience often triggers in them strong feelings of loss that they turn into anger against themselves, which sometimes manifests itself as depression or withdrawal. But people cope with such situations in diverse ways. After a short period of mourning their losses, some bounce back (having learned something) and adapt successfully; others get permanently stuck in bitter and self-destructive positions.

Those who do not recover from severe disappointment often find themselves stuck in no-exit jobs that they do not enjoy and are not particularly proud of. They find it difficult to accept that their careers have

plateaued in this way. They feel cheated. The emotional
tension of an unenjoyable job, now aggravated by bitterness, often spills over into their home lives, where everyone else also pays for their sense of failure. Private life, as
well as professional life, becomes hollow and empty. The
injury to self-esteem they received in the professional
world seems to color their whole experience of life.

Other plateaued managers recover their enthusiasm
for their professional and private lives in a constructive
way. They may compensate for their disappointment by
enriching their present jobs—for example, adopting a
role as mentor.

Often this positive compensation comes through
developing leisure activities. These activities have, however, a professional quality to them rather than being
mere relaxation. One man transformed his hobby of riding into a weekend riding school. Another got involved
in community activities. A third broadened his home
redecorating pastime into buying, redoing, and selling
old houses. In these examples, work became more meaningful in that it helped to finance an active leisure interest; family life benefited since the man recovered his
sense of self-esteem.

We can add a nuance to Freud's idea that the main
sources of self-esteem and pleasure in an individual's life
are work and love. Failure at work cannot be fully compensated by success in love. Failure at work has to be
compensated by success in worklike activities. Only
when work and love coexist in parallel and appropriate
proportions do we achieve happiness and fulfillment.

What Organizations Can Do

We have suggested that the main responsibility for managing a career, reducing negative spillover, and achieving

a good balance between professional and private life lies with the individual executive. It makes more sense for individuals to feel responsible for managing their own professional lives (taking care that career does not destroy private life) than to expect the organization to do this for them. Management in organizations, however, bears the responsibility for practices and policies that may make it unnecessarily difficult for the individual executive to manage the relationship between his professional and private lives. We see four things top managers can do to reduce the work pressures.

BROADEN ORGANIZATIONAL VALUES

Our first recommendation to managers is likely to be the most heretical. Managers can help their people by encouraging them not to be devoted solely to career success. Many managers attach too high a value to effort, drive, dedication, dynamism, and energy. Managers often take long hours at work and apparent single-minded dedication to professional success as indicators of drive and ambition. Attachment to private life and efforts to protect it by working "only" 45 hours a week are interpreted as signs of weakness in today's middle aged; in younger managers, this pattern signifies an erosion of the work ethic, a symptom of what is wrong with the younger generation.

We find little evidence in our research, however, of an erosion of the work ethic among younger managers. Their professional commitment is strong, but it represents a commitment to what interests them rather than a blind commitment to their companies. They resist simply doing what has to be done and conforming to organizational practices, even if they are compensated by incentives. They are aware that a lot of office time is wasted by engaging in ritualistic, nonproductive "work" and that few people make a real success of activities that fail to excite and interest them. Above all they appreciate that the quality of an individual's work life has an enormous impact, positive or negative, on his private life.

Paradoxically, organizations do not necessarily work better when they are full of highly ambitious, career-centered individuals striving to get to the top. As a matter of fact, these "jungle fighters" are often ostracized by their colleagues and superiors because they have too much ambition and too little ability to work with others. What organizations ideally need are a few ambitious and talented high achievers (who fit with their jobs) and a majority of balanced, less ambitious but conscientious people more interested in doing a good job that they enjoy and are adequately rewarded for than in climbing the organizational pyramid.

Organizational practices that overvalue effort and climbing and undervalue pride in one's job and good performance are counterproductive. Economic recessions in years to come will make this even more apparent. As the growth rates of organizations stabilize, the possibilities for advancement and promotion will diminish. People will be productive only if they enjoy the intrinsic value of what they are doing and if they draw their satisfaction simultaneously from two sources—work and private life—instead of one.

CREATE MULTIPLE REWARD AND CAREER LADDERS

Since external rewards often pressure people into accepting jobs they don't fit, our second recommendation concerns the reward policies and ladders of organizations.

The reward ladder of most organizations is a very simple, one-dimensional hierarchy; the higher, the more "managerial" one is, the more one is rewarded. People come to equate success with the managerial ladder, which would be appropriate if skilled managerial people were the only skilled people we need. But this is far from the case. Most organizations have relatively few general managerial positions and, while these are important posts, the life blood of the company is provided by people who fit with their jobs in other ways. To encourage these people, reward ladders need to be far more differentiated than they are at present.

Edgar H. Schein shows how managers fit with their work and careers in at least five different ways that he calls "career anchors."[4] While some people indeed have managerial anchors (that is, they aspire to positions in general management), others are oriented toward expertise in a technical or functional area. A desire to be creative is the central motive in the careers of a third group. (And do we not need more entrepreneurs in our large organizations today?) The fourth and fifth groups are anchored in needs for security and autonomy, respectively.

The obvious implication is that organizations must create multiple career and reward ladders to develop the different types of people required for their operations. Some high technology companies that rely heavily on technical innovation have indeed experimented with offering both managerial and technical reward ladders. In the future, we will probably see the development of reward ladders that reinforce creativity and entrepreneurship as well.

The problem with the simple structures of many organizations is that they channel ambition and talent in only one direction, creating unnecessary conflict for the many individuals who are ambitious or talented but do not walk the single prescribed path. We can warn individuals against being blinded by ambition to the emotional aspects of fit; yet we we must also warn organizations, not against fostering ambition, but against channeling it into a single career path.

GIVE REALISTIC PERFORMANCE APPRAISALS

Our third recommendation is that managers help individuals in their own self-assessment, thus reducing the chances that they will either move into positions that do not fit them or be promoted to their "Peter Principle" level of incompetence. To do this, managers need to pay greater attention to their subordinates' performances and also to be honest in discussions of the subordinates' strengths and weaknesses. Managers should also encourage self-assessment. Contrary to standard assessment practices that only emphasize skills and competence, self-assessment should focus as well on the extent to which the individual enjoys his job—both as a whole and in its component parts.

Many researchers have called for accurate and realistic feedback in performance appraisal.[5] We also ask that managers be as concerned and realistic about enjoyment and value as about competence.

Of all managerial omissions, lack of candor about a subordinate's chances for promotion can be most destructive. At one time or another, to one degree or another, most managers have agonized over trying to motivate an individual with the lure of promotion while knowing that the individual does not have much of a chance. Candor may result in employees' short-term unhappiness and even in their leaving the company, but we suggest that the long-run effects of dissembling are far worse. Eventually truth will out, and the negative effects of disappointment are likely to harm not only the individual's performance at work but also, through the spillover effect, his private life—at a time when perhaps it's too late for him to change jobs.

REDUCE ORGANIZATIONAL UNCERTAINTY

Uncertainty is an increasingly frequent fixture of today's world. Sudden, unpredictable events—like an oil shortage or the taking of hostages in Iran—can have massive impact on the lives of managers in Dallas, Paris, or Bogotá. Economic recession lurks in the background, and no one feels entirely safe. The jobless executive next door makes many a manager aware that "it could also happen to me." Reorganization and restructuring of companies have become almost annual events; and sudden policy changes have vast repercussions on people's lives that create worries and preoccupations and lead to emotional spillover.

Managers can help reduce unnecessary stress and uncertainty by protecting their subordinates from worry about events over which they have no control. A good example of this is the young manager of a foreign exchange department in a large bank. It is difficult to imagine a more uncertain, hectic, anxiety-ridden job. When we asked him how he managed, he answered: "I protect my subordinates and I trust them. When my superiors drop by to tell us how stupid what we did yesterday was and ask who did it, I tell them that it's none of their business. I offer them my job if they want it. That shuts them up quite fast."

We asked him how he could trust his subordinates in a department that could lose millions in a day. He answered: "I trust them because I have to. And I have learned to show them that I trust them by leaving them alone to do their jobs and helping them only when they ask for help."

Here we have a "shock-absorbing" manager. However, the price for his courage is enormous. He absorbs a lot of the anxiety around him, acting as a buffer against many pressures. He has an ulcer and no nails, but his subordinates love him.

Top managers cannot expect to have many people like this in their ranks. But they clearly need people who can absorb as many shocks for others as possible. And they owe it to such people to relieve them from positions where uncertainty is too high by systematically rotating these jobs after a certain time. People can protect others from uncertainty and anxiety (to some extent this is part of a manager's job), but only for so long.

Whose Life Is It Anyway?

In managerial circles, there's something almost sacred about the separation between private and professional life. The respect for an individual's privacy is one of our fundamental values. However, no one can deny that work has a powerful effect on private life. The issue is where does responsible behavior stop and where does interference begin?

The individual executive adheres to the principle that his private life is none of the organization's business. But today he does expect the organization asking him to accept a big new job in Latin America to consider as legitimate his concerns about, say, his three children and his wife with her own career. In the interest of his future performance, the corporation is well advised to listen and respond to his concerns.

We do not need to invoke altruism to recommend that organizations make sure their people are in jobs that fit them, that they can cope with the changes the organization may ask of them, and that they have the tools for realistic self-assessment. Doing this is essential to the morale and productivity of the organization.

Responsible behavior on the part of the organization is simply behavior that is in its own best interest. This means recognizing the emotional aspects of work and career. A person's capacity to enjoy doing a job is as important a consideration as his potential competence.

Even if organizations choose not to deal with these issues, the changing values and life-styles of younger managers—especially those in dual-career marriages—may eventually force top management to face the impact work has on private life.

Notes

1. See our article, "Professional Lives Versus Private Lives—Shifting Patterns of Managerial Commitment," *Organizational Dynamics*, Spring 1979, p. 2.

2. *Ibid.*

3. Abraham Zaleznik, "Management of Disappointment," HBR, November–December, 1967, p. 59.

4. Edgar H. Schein, *Career Dynamics* (Reading, MA: Addison-Wesley, 1978).

5. See, for example, Harry Levinson, "Emotional Health in the World of Work" in *Management by Guilt* (New York: Harper & Row, 1964), pp. 267–291.

Originally published in March–April 1980
Reprint 80203

Authors' note: The ideas described in this article are the result of many hours of conversation with executives and their wives. Both of us are conducting research on the relationship between the professional and private lives of male executives; our extensive questionnaire has been completed by 700 international managers. The quotations are taken directly from interviews conducted with 44 executive couples in the United Kingdom and France and from exchanges with more than 2,000 executives of many different nationalities who attended executive development courses and seminars at the European Institute of Business Administration over a period of five years.

When Executives Burn Out

HARRY LEVINSON

Executive Summary

"IN MY ROLE, I'm the guy who catches it all. I can't seem to get people to stand still and listen, and I can't continue to take all the hostility. I don't know how much longer I can last in this job."

The executive who speaks these words is one of several who describe their feelings of burnout in this HBR Classic, first published in May–June 1981. In addition to feeling anger, cynicism, and helplessness, burned-out managers—those who expend a great deal of effort without visible results—often suffer from physical symptoms such as headaches, chronic fatigue, and an inability to shake colds. Anyone can feel overwhelmed by the challenges posed by complex organizations and the need to deal with conflicting personalities, says psychologist Harry Levinson. In this article, he suggests ways in which top management can help prevent burnout. For example,

it can rotate executives out of potentially exhausting positions, provide avenues through which they can freely
express their frustrations, retrain them and upgrade their
skills, and offer them opportunities for physical recreation.
In his retrospective commentary, Levinson notes that
although burnout is as prevalent today as it was 15
years ago, the assumption underlying his article—that top
management can play a role in preventing burnout—now
feels outdated. (See "A New Age of Self-Reliance" at
the end of this article.) Why? Because we are living in
an age of self-reliance. Now that most companies no
longer expect to have long-term relationships with their
employees, workers—even executives—must not become
too dependent on any one job or employer. Instead of
acquiring specific skills, Levinson says, we need to tap
into our characteristic behaviors to develop career alternatives. If the work we do is at the core of who we are,
our stress level will go down.

"**I** JUST CAN'T SEEM TO GET GOING," the vice president said. He grimaced as he leaned back in his chair.
"I can't get interested in what I'm supposed to do. I
know I should get rolling. I know there's a tremendous
amount of work to be done. That's why they brought
me in and put me in this job, but I just can't seem to
get going."

Eighteen months before making these comments, the
vice president had transferred to company headquarters
from a subsidiary. His new job was to revamp the company's control systems, which, because of a reorganization, were in disarray. When the vice president reported

to headquarters, however, top management immediately recruited him to serve as a key staff figure in its own reshuffling. Because he was not in competition with line executives, he was the only staff person who interviewed and consulted with both the line executives and the chief executive officer. And because the top managers regarded him as trustworthy, they gave his recommendations serious attention.

But his task had been arduous. Not only did the long hours and the unremitting pressure of walking a tightrope among conflicting interests exhaust him; they also made it impossible for him to get at the control problems that needed attention. Furthermore, because his family could not move until his youngest child finished high school, he commuted on weekends to his family's home 800 miles away. As he tried to perform the job that had been thrust on him and to support the CEO, who was counting heavily on his competence, he felt lonely, harassed, and burdened. Now that his staff responsibilities were coming to an end, he was in no psychological shape to take on his formal duties. In short, he had "burned out."

Like generalized stress, burnout cuts across executive and managerial levels. While the phenomenon manifests itself in varying ways and to different degrees in different people, it appears nonetheless to have identifiable characteristics. For instance, in the next example, the individual is different but many of the features of the problem are the same.

A vice president of a large corporation who hadn't received an expected promotion left his company to become the CEO of a smaller, family-owned business, which was floundering and needed his skills. Although he had jumped at the opportunity to rescue the small company, once there he discovered an unimaginable morass of difficulties, among them continual conflicts within the family. He felt he could not leave, but neither could he succeed. Trapped in a kind of psychological quicksand, he worked days, nights, and weekends for months in an attempt to pull himself free. His wife protested, to no avail. Finally, he was hospitalized for exhaustion.

As in the previous example, the competence of the individual is not in question; today he is the chief executive of a major corporation.

Quite a different set of problems confronted another executive. This is how he tells his story:

"In March of 1963, I moved to a small town in Iowa with my wife and son of four weeks. I was an up-and-coming engineer with the electric company—magic and respected words in those days.

"Ten years later, things had changed. When we went to social gatherings and talked to people, I ended up having to defend the electric company. At the time, we were tying into a consortium that was building a nuclear generating plant. The amount of negative criticism was immense, and it never really let up. Refusing to realize how important that generating plant was to a reliable flow of electricity, people continued to find fault.

"In my role, I'm the guy who catches it all. I don't know how much longer I can last in this job."

"Now, nearly ten years later, we are under even greater attack. In my present role, I'm the guy who catches it all. I can't seem to get people to stand still and listen, and I can't continue to take all the hostility that goes with it—the crank calls, being woken up late at night and called names. I don't know how much longer I can last in this job."

Before looking in depth at what the phenomenon of burnout is, let's look at the experience of one more executive who is well on his way to burning out: "I have been with this company for nearly 15 years and have changed jobs every 2 to 3 years. Most of our managers are company men, like me. We have always been a high-technology company, but we have been doing less well in marketing than some of our competitors have. Over the past 10 years, we have been going through a continuous reorganization process. The organization charts keep changing, but the underlying philosophy, management techniques, and administrative trappings don't. The consequence is continuous frustration, disruption, resentment, and the undermining of 'change.' You don't take a company that has been operating with a certain perspective and turn it around overnight.

"With these changes, we are also being told what we must do and when. Before, we were much more flexible and free to follow our noses. These shifts create enormous pressures on an organization that is used to different ways of operating.

"On top of that, a continual corporate pruning goes on. I am a survivor, so I should feel good about it and believe what top management tells me, namely, that the unfit go and the worthy remain. But the old virtues—talent, initiative, and risk taking—are *not* being rewarded. Instead, acquiescence to corporate values and social skills that obliterate differences among individuals are the virtues that get attention. Also, the reward process is more political than meritocratic.

"I don't know if we're going to make it. And there are a lot of others around here who have the same feeling. We're all demoralized."

Burnout—A Slow Fizzle

What was happening to these executives? In exploring that question, let's first look at what characterized the situations. In one or more cases, the situations

• were repetitive or prolonged;

• placed enormous burdens on the managers;

• promised great success but made attaining it nearly impossible;

• exposed the managers to risk of attack for doing their jobs, without providing a way for them to fight back;

• aroused deep emotions—sorrow, fear, despair, compassion, helplessness, pity, and rage; to survive, the managers would try to contain their feelings and hide their anguish;

• overwhelmed the managers with complex detail, conflicting forces, and problems against which they hurled themselves with increasing intensity but without impact;

• exploited the managers but provided them little to show for having been victimized;

• aroused an inescapable sense of inadequacy and often of guilt;

• left the managers feeling that no one knew, let alone gave a damn about, what price they were paying, what contribution or sacrifice they were making, or what punishment they were absorbing;

- caused the managers to raise the question What for?—as if they'd lost sight of the purpose of living.

Those who study cases like these agree that a special phenomenon occurs after people expend a great deal of effort, intense to the point of exhaustion, without visible results. People in these situations feel angry, helpless, trapped, and depleted: they are burned out. This experience is more intense than what is ordinarily referred to as stress. The major defining characteristic of burnout is that people can't or won't do again what they have been doing.

Herbert J. Freudenberger, a New York psychologist, evolved this characterization of burnout when he observed a special sort of fatigue among mental health workers.[1] Freudenberger observed that burnout is associated with physiological signs such as frequent headaches and the inability to shake colds, as well as with psychological symptoms such as quickness to anger and a suspicious attitude about others.

Christina Maslach, a pioneer researcher on the subject at the University of California at Berkeley, says that burnout "refers to a syndrome of emotional exhaustion and cynicism that frequently occurs among people who do 'people work'—who spend considerable time in close encounters."[2]

People suffering from burnout generally have these identifiable characteristics: (1) chronic fatigue; (2) anger at those making demands; (3) self-criticism for putting up with the demands; (4) cynicism, negativity, and irritability; (5) a sense of being besieged; and (6) hair-trigger display of emotions.

Although it is not evident from the above examples, a wide range of behaviors—some of them destructive—frequently accompany these feelings. Burned-out managers may inappropriately vent anger at subordinates and family, or withdraw even from those whose support they need the most. They may wall off home and work from each other completely. They may try to escape the source of pressure through illness, absenteeism, or drugs or alcohol, or by seeking temporary psychological refuge in meditation, biofeedback, or other forms of self-hypnosis. They may display increasingly rigid attitudes or appear cold and detached.

Most people, even effective managers, probably experience a near burnout at some time in their careers. A 20-year study of a group of middle managers disclosed that many of them, now in their forties and with few prospects of further promotions, were tolerating unhappy marriages, narrowing their focus to their own jobs, and showing less consideration toward other people.[3] Despite outward sociability, they were indifferent to friendships and often hostile. They had become rigid, had short fuses, and were distant from their children.

Personality tests disclosed that these managers had a greater need to do a job well for its own sake than did most of their peers and that they initially had a greater need for advancement as well (although it declined over time). They showed more motivation to dominate and lead, and less to defer to authority than other managers. While they still could do a good day's work, they could no longer invest themselves in others and in the company.

The manager must cope with the least capable, the suspicious, the rivalrous, the self-centered, and the generally unhappy.

When people who feel an intense need to achieve don't reach their goals, they can become hostile to themselves and to others. They also tend to channel that hostility into more defined work tasks than before, limiting their efforts. If at times like these they do not increase their involvement in family matters, they are likely to approach burnout.

The Breeding Ground

Researchers have observed this type of exhaustion among many kinds of professionals. As the examples here indicate, it is not unusual among executives and managers, and it is more likely to occur under competitive conditions than in a stable market. Managerial jobs involve a lot of contact with other people. Often this contact is unpleasant but has to be tolerated because of the inherent demands of the job.

One problem with managing people is that such a focus creates unending stress for the manager. The manager must cope with the least capable of the employees, with the depressed, the suspicious, the rivalrous, the self-centered, and the generally unhappy. The manager must balance these conflicting personalities and create from them a motivated work group. He or she must define group purpose and organize people around it, as well as resolve conflicts, establish priorities, make decisions about other people, accept and deflect their hostility, and deal with the frustration that arises out of that continuing interaction. Managing people is the most difficult administrative task, and it has built-in

As more women join the workforce, the support most men used to receive at home is lessening.

frustration. That frustration can—and does—cause many managers to burn out. Many contemporary managerial situations also provide the perfect breeding ground for cases of burnout. Today's managers face increasing time pressures with little respite. Even though benefits such as flexible working hours and longer vacations offer some relief, for the most part the modern executive's workday is long and hard. Also, as more women join the workforce, the support most men used to receive at home is lessening, and women who work get as little support as, if not less support than, the men. To many managers, the time they spend with their families is precious. It is understandable if managers feel guilty about sacrificing this part of their life to the demands of work and if they also feel frustration at being unable to do anything about it.

Adding to the stress at work is the complexity of modern organizations. The bigger and more intricate organizations become, the longer it takes to get things done. Managers trying to get ahead may well feel enormous frustration as each person or office a project passes through adds more delays and more problems to unravel before a task is finished.

Along with the increasing complexity of organizations goes an increase in the number of people that a manager has to deal with. Participative management, quality-of-work-life efforts, and matrix structures all result in a proliferation in the number of people that a manager must confront face-to-face. Building a plant, developing natural resources, or designing new products can often mean that a manager has to go through lengthy, and sometimes angry and vitriolic, interaction with community groups. Executives involved in tasks that entail controversial issues may find themselves vilified.

As companies grow, merge with other companies, or go through reorganizations, some managers feel as though they are adrift. Sacrifices they have made on behalf of the organization may well turn out to have little enduring meaning. As an organization's values change, a manager's commitment and sense of support may also shift. Another aspect of change that can add to a feeling of burnout is the threat of obsolescence. When a new position or assignment requires that managers who are already feeling taxed develop new skills, they may feel overwhelmed.

These days, change can also mean that managers have to trim jobs and demote subordinates—or maybe even discharge them. Managers whose job it is to close a plant or to go through painful labor negotiations may feel enraged at having to pay for the sins of their predecessors. Also, a fragmented marketplace can mean intense pressures on managers to come up with new products, innovative services, and novel marketing and financing schemes.

Finally, employees are making increasing demands for their rights. Managers may feel that they cannot satisfy those demands but have to respond to them nevertheless.

Prevention Is the Best Cure

Top management can take steps to keep managers out of situations in which they are likely to burn out. Of course, something as subtle as psychological exhaustion cannot be legislated against completely, but acting on the following insights can help mitigate its occurrence:

First, as with all such phenomena, recognize that burnout can, does, and will happen. The people in charge of orientation programs, management training courses, and discussions of managerial practice ought to acknowledge to employees that burnout can occur and that people's vulnerability to it is something the organization recognizes and cares about. Personnel managers should be candid with new employees about the psychological aspects of the work they are getting into, especially when that work involves intense effort of the kind I've described. The more people know, the less guilt they are likely to feel about their own perceived inadequacies when the pressures begin to mount.

Don't allow the same people to be the rescuers of troubled situations over and over again.

Keep track of how long your subordinates are in certain jobs and rotate them out of potentially exhausting positions. Changes of pace, changes of demands, and shifts into situations that may not be so depleting enable people to replenish their energies and get new and more accurate perspectives on themselves and their roles. Change also enables people to look forward to a time when they can get out of a binding job. Long recognizing this need, the military limits the number of combat missions that air force personnel fly and the duration of tours that ground personnel must serve.

Time constraints on a job are crucial to preventing burnout. Don't allow your people to work 18 hours a day, even on critical problems. Especially don't let the same people be the rescuers of troubled situations over and over again. Understandably, managers tend to rely on their best people; but the best people are more vulnerable to becoming burned-out people. The overconscientious, in particular, need to take time off from the demands of their role and to spend that time in refreshing recreation. The military has learned this lesson, but

management has not. One way to make sure people
break from work is to take the whole group on a nominal
business trip to a recreational site.

Some companies have set up regular formal retreats
where people who work together under pressure can talk
about what they are doing and how they are doing it,
make long-range plans,
relax and enjoy them-
selves, and, most impor-
tant, get away from what
they have to cope with
every day. When man-
agers talk together in a setting like this, they are able to
make realistic assessments of the problems they are up
against and their own responsibilities and limitations.

*Many performance review
programs actually contribute
to a sense that one's
efforts will be unrecognized.*

I think, for example, of the extremely conscientious
engineers in many of the small electronics companies on
Route 128 in the Boston area, and of those in the
research triangle in North Carolina or in the Palo Alto,
California, area, who have reported feeling that they simply are not developing new products fast enough. They
are convinced that they aren't living up to the extremely
high standards that they set for themselves. Such people
need to talk together, often with a group therapist or
someone else who can help them let go of some of the
irrational demands they frequently make on themselves
as groups and as individuals.

Make sure your organization has a systematic way of
letting people know that their contributions are important. People need information that supports their positive self-image, eases their conscience, and refuels them
psychologically. Many compensation and performance
appraisal programs actually contribute to people's sense
that their efforts will be unrecognized no matter how

well they do. Organizational structures and processes that inhibit timely attacks on problems and delay competitive actions can produce much of the stress that people feel at work. If top executives fail to see that organizational factors can cause burnout, their lack of understanding may perpetuate the problem.

It is also important that top-level managers review with people their capacities, skills, and opportunities so that, armed with facts about themselves and the organization, they can make choices rather than feel trapped.

During World War II, the army discovered that it was better to send soldiers overseas in groups rather than as single replacements. It may be equally effective for managers to send groups of people from one organizational task to another rather than assemble teams of individually assigned people. When Clairol opened a new plant in California, it sent out a group of Connecticut-based managers and their spouses, who were briefed on the new assignment, the new community, and the potential stresses they might encounter. The managers discussed how they might help themselves and one another, as well as what support they needed from the organization. People who have worked together have already established mutual support systems, ways to share knowledge informally, and friendly alliances. These can prevent or ameliorate the burnout that may occur in new, difficult, or threatening tasks.

Managers should provide avenues through which people can express not only their anger but also their disappointment, helplessness, hopelessness, defeat, and depression. Some employees, such as salespeople, meet defeat every day. Others meet defeat in a crisis—when a major contract is lost, when a product expected to succeed fails, when the competition outflanks them. When people in defeat deny their angry feelings, that denial of underlying, seething anger contributes to the sense of burnout.

If top executives fail to see these problems as serious, they may worsen the situation. If a company offers only palliatives like meditation and relaxation methods— temporarily helpful though they may be—victims of burnout may become further enraged. The sufferers know that their problem has to do with the nature of the job and not their capacity to handle it.

Those managers who are exposed to attack need to talk about the hostilities they anticipate and how to cope with them. Just as sailors at sea need to anticipate and cope with storms, so executives need to learn how to cope with the public's aggression. Under attack themselves, they need to develop consensus, foster cohesion, and build trust rather than undermine themselves through counterattacks.

Another way executives can help is by defending the organization publicly against outside attacks. For example, a prominent chief executive once raised the morale of all his employees when he filed suit against a broadcast medium for making false allegations about his company's products. Another publicly took on a newspaper that had implied his organization was not trustworthy. A visible, vigorous, and powerful leader does much to counteract people's sense of helplessness.

As technology changes, you need to retrain and upgrade your managers. But some people will be unable to rise to new levels of responsibility and are likely to feel defeated if they cannot succeed in the same job. Top management needs to retrain, refresh, and reinvigorate these managers as quickly as possible by getting them to seminars, workshops, and other activities away from the organization.

As Freudenberger commented after his early observations, however, introspection is not what the burned-out person requires; rather, he or she needs intense physical activity, not further mental strain and fatigue. Retreats, seminars, and workshops therefore should be oriented toward the physical rather than the emotional. Physical exercise is helpful because it provides a healthy outlet for angry feelings and pent-up energy.

Managers who are burning out need support from others who can offer psychological sustenance. Ideally, those others should be their supervisors—people who value them as individuals and insist that they withdraw, get appropriate help, and place themselves first. In times of unmitigated strain, it is particularly important for managers to keep up personal interaction with their subordinates. To borrow from the military again, generals valued by their troops, such as George Patton and James Gavin in World War II, have made it a practice to be involved with their frontline soldiers.

Freudenberger points out that the burnout phenomenon often occurs when a leader or the leader's charisma is lost. He notes that people who join an organization still led by the founder or founding group frequently expect that person or group to be superhuman. After all, the entrepreneurs had the foresight, vision, drive, and imagination to build the organization. "As they begin to disappoint us, we bad-rap them, and the result, unless it is stopped, is psychic damage to the whole clinic," he comments.[4] The issue is the same for a clinic, a hospital, a police department, or a business.

Executives who are idealized should take time to remove their halos in public. They can do that by explaining their own struggles, disappointments, and defeats to their subordinates so that the latter can view them more accurately. They also need to help people verbalize their disappointment with the "fallen" executive hero.

When the leader leaves, through either death or transfer, when a paternalistic and successful entrepreneur sells out, or when an imaginative inventor retires, it is important for the group that remains to have the opportunity to go through a process of discussing its loss and mourning it. The group needs to conduct its own psychological wake and consider for itself how it is going to deal with the loss.

Frequently, the group will discover that, although the loss of the leader is indeed significant, it can carry on effectively and contribute to the organization's success. Failing to realize its own strengths, a group can, like the Green Bay Packers after the loss of coach Vince Lombardi, feel permanently handicapped. To my knowledge, few organizations deal effectively with the loss of a leader. Most respond with a depression or slump from which it takes years to recover. Even more crippling is the way people in the organization keep yearning and searching for a new charismatic leader to rescue them. As part of a national organization, Americans have been doing this searching ever since the death of John Kennedy.

A New Age of Self-Reliance
by Harry Levinson

FIFTEEN YEARS AGO, executive burnout was a new phenomenon. Not so anymore. Today extreme feelings of stress are pervasive and growing worse. Reengineering, downsizing, and increased competition have multiplied pressures in the workplace. At the same time, dual-earner couples suffer time and energy famines at home. In the 1990s, it is hard to find peace anywhere.

When I wrote "When Executives Burn Out" in 1981, a chief underlying assumption was that senior management had a role to play in preventing executive burnout. My advice in the article reflected that proposition, and I suggested actions that leaders could take to prevent stress, such as supplying recreation and offering training.

This basic assumption now feels outdated. Why? Because the forces changing the world in which we work and live have also changed the relationship between the employer and the employee. As we read in the paper every day, most companies no longer expect to have long-term relationships with their employees. In turn, workers—even executives—make sure that they are not too dependent on any one job or employer. They no longer look to the employer to support them. They now look to themselves.

A psychological and practical result of these changes is that we are living in a new age of self-reliance. On a personal level, we must get feedback, advice, and moral support from family and friends. On a professional level, we each need to develop fallback positions. By *fallback*, I mean an alternative course of action if the current job fails us. In today's world, we need to worry less about the next rung up the ladder and more about the variety of possibilities available to us should the ladder disappear and we find ourselves thrown back on our own resources.

In developing our careers, most of us have thought in terms of acquiring specific competencies (such as marketing techniques, financial analysis skills, or engineering specialization). Of course, skills are necessary, but they will make little difference to us as the tools of our trade if they become outdated. A specific skill will never be an enduring source of self-reliance, because it risks losing its value in the marketplace.

To develop attractive and realistic career alternatives, we need to think more in terms of our characteristic behaviors. We must understand the behaviors that we have developed since childhood, patterns that express *who we are* instead of what we do. Whether we are naturally levelheaded, spontaneously enthusiastic, artlessly charming, or born to persevere, we take our behaviors with us into everything we do. If what you do is at the core of who you are, your stress level will go down.

In developing your fallback positions, think about what you do spontaneously. The great entertainer Myron Cohen became a comedian because he was frustrated working in the garment business but was good at telling jokes to his friends. A few years ago, we all read about a successful financier who honored his inborn musical talents by becoming a respected conductor. We hear every day about successful businesspeople who "chuck it all" to satisfy their deeper need to be an artist, teacher, minister, or builder of affordable housing. These people will never want to retire, because they are acting on who they truly are.

Understanding and tapping into your most characteristic behaviors will give you more security and less stress than anything else you can do. To believe otherwise is to ignore reality.

Notes

1. Herbert J. Freudenberger, "Staff Burn-Out," *Journal of Social Issues*, vol. 30, no. 1, 1974, p. 159; see also his book

Burn-Out: The Melancholy of High Achievement (New York: Doubleday, 1980).

2. Christina Maslach, "Burn-Out," *Human Behavior*, September 1976, p. 16.

3. Douglas W. Bray, Richard J. Campbell, and Donald L. Grant, *Formative Years in Business* (New York: John Wiley, 1974).

4. Freudenberger, "Staff Burn-Out," p. 160.

Originally published in July–August 1996
Reprint 96406

This article was originally published in May–June 1981, and it won second place in that year's McKinsey Awards. For its republication as an HBR Classic, Harry Levinson has written the commentary "A New Age of Self-Reliance" to update his observations and advice.

The Work Alibi

When It's Harder to Go Home

FERNANDO BARTOLOMÉ

Executive Summary

LACK OF TIME is one of the best excuses for not doing almost anything. Because all of us use it, we're all ready to believe it. But if you do some simple calculations, the author of this article points out, you'll find that the amount of time most executives spend at work isn't more than half of their waking hours. If lack of time isn't the cause of the unsatisfactory home lives that worry many of them, what is? The author explores some important contributing factors to a disappointing personal life, such as having the wrong assumptions in the first place, being excessively afraid of confronting conflict, and taking a "mañana" approach to problems. He concludes, however, that the most important factors are a married couple's ability to maintain an ongoing dialogue about their feelings, to ask openly for what they truly need from each other, and to have fun.

81

IN DISCUSSIONS WITH EXECUTIVES about how they mesh their personal and business lives, I hear versions of the following story countless times.

"We married when we were young. We had very little experience in dealing with personal problems and so we had troubles from the beginning. We didn't know how to talk about how we felt. We'd get angry at each other and sometimes we'd argue, but never constructively. We thought it would get better, but it didn't. When we had our first child, things seemed easier between us. Then we had our second one—a boy. Our marriage still wasn't good—we couldn't talk about our problems—but we loved our kids. Then we found out that the boy had a congenital heart problem.

"It was just about then that my father retired and I took over the family business. I worked a lot and when we talked, it was always about little Johnny. We stopped even trying to talk about our own problems. The boy got worse. Finally we had to operate, and he died. The pain was terrible. That brought us closer, but still we couldn't talk. I needed something else. I fell in love with another woman. Three years later I divorced my wife."

What I hear so often is a story of the tragedy and waste that can afflict the personal lives of many successful executives because of lack of attention and skill. In these conversations I find executives searching for a solution to difficult and painful problems at home and for ways to reinvigorate their private lives.

In general, executives' private lives are not in terrible shape. Most people, however, have unresolved personal problems that worry them and often a feeling that "something is missing." For some the issue may be a concern with a child. Others feel that their marriages have lost vitality. Many worry about their life style or physical health. It is dealing with such problems that executives often find difficult.

When I ask executives why their private lives are not as fulfilling as they would like them to be, most answer that they lack time and energy for personal affairs because of their devotion to work. And when I ask them how they feel about this, most of them say they feel "guilty." Their use of the word guilty is revealing. It implies that they feel they are at least partly responsible for this situation through neglect.

While in some cases work may contribute to an unsatisfactory family life, in many others it becomes an alibi that executives use to cover up much more important factors.

When Work Is to Blame

Let's talk first about those cases when work does contribute to a poor private life. Strong and persistent negative emotional spillover that a stressful work situation can produce is sure to cause havoc at home.[1] But absence of spillover is not enough to ensure that time at home is happy. A well-functioning professional life is a necessary but not a sufficient condition for a good private life: an executive may be available to family and friends, but availability doesn't automatically make him or her a good parent, spouse, or companion.

Another way in which professional life can have a negative effect on the home is when executives work too much. "Workaholism" is one type of overwork. The word, with its connotation rooted in "alcoholism," implies escape or avoidance of problems through a drug, in this case, work. Despite the similar consequences—an

estranged family and impaired health—society con-
demns alcoholism but condones and even applauds
workaholism.

But while many people who work excessively are
workaholics, others whose actions may produce the
same effects are simply "prisoners of success." The difference between the workaholic and the prisoner of success
is that while the former is trying to escape through over
involvement in work, the latter has simply fallen in love
with the job and the rewards it brings. Executives
addicted to success don't escape their private lives but
simply neglect them.

Popular belief to the contrary, if the executive population I interviewed is representative, workaholics and prisoners of success are the exception rather than the rule.

When I ask executives to estimate what proportion of
their waking hours they invest in work, most estimate
between 60% and 70% per week. Yet when I do some
arithmetic, I usually find a number much closer to 50%
(see the exhibit "Work Isn't the Real Problem"). These
figures hold for a great majority of managers and executives, and they would be even lower if I included in my
calculations vacation time and holidays. In any event,
explaining family difficulties in terms of pressures of
work doesn't hold water. The time that most executives
have available for their private lives is roughly equal to, if
not greater than, the time they devote to work.

For most executives, therefore, the only way work can
have a direct negative influence on private life is through
negative emotional spillover. But when spillover is
absent and an executive's private life is still not as good
as he or she would wish, the causes have to be found
elsewhere.

If It's Not Work, What Is It?

My discussions with many executives have helped me identify a number of factors that hurt their private lives. These include: incorrect assumptions, excessive fear of confronting conflicts in marriage, legitimate distractions, a "mañana" attitude, and, in general, a lack of necessary skills.

INCORRECT ASSUMPTIONS

The most pervasive wrong assumption executives hold is that managing family life is easy—something they can do

---

Work Isn't the Real Problem

The calculations for a typical week are simple

Total available hours	24 hours × 7 days =	**168**	
Minus average sleep	7 hours × 7 days =	49	
Total waking hours		**119**	100%
Working hours			
Average time at the office	9 hours × 5 days =	45	
Average time commuting	2 hours × 5 days =	10	
Average work time during weekends		4	
Total work time		**59**	49.57%

Note: A 10-hour work day would result in total work time of 64 hours, that is, 53.78% of total waking hours spent working.

---

with their left hands while their right hands are busy
dealing with their professional lives.

Executives have formal training to be accountants,
financial analysts, marketing specialists, or computer
experts; many professionals must have a diploma to
practice. Yet, despite all the evidence to the contrary,
many managers assume that they can learn to be good
spouses without thinking about it or developing the
necessary skills. People get married with neither full
awareness of the problems that can arise in a marriage
nor the skills necessary to establish an intimate relationship that is intended to be exclusive and last a
lifetime.

When I mention this lack of training to executives,
many respond that, "You can't study those things. You
learn them by trial and error." But is this really so? Consider business affairs. Even though management is still
largely an art, executives haven't stopped learning analytical concepts and processes that have proved helpful
in understanding problems and identifying opportunities. The same should apply to private life.

Some people assume that it is easy to love their children. But while we may not have to learn to feel the emotion we call love, it is often very difficult to learn to love
children in the "right" way, or to educate and raise them.
We can't learn these things in a hurry when crises arrive;
we need to learn them over time in a persistent way,
which takes energy, commitment, and the gradual development of necessary skills.

I have seen many competent men and women executives who accept the challenge of professional problems
throw up their arms in despair when the solution to a
problem with a child doesn't come easily to them. One
executive's description of his frustration is typical:

"I feel extremely competent at work, but not at home. At home I feel like a bumbling idiot. For example, I relate very well to one of my kids, almost too well; he is very fond of me and I think he may be excessively dependent on me. He is my oldest. My youngest kid is exactly the opposite. He is very independent and seems to avoid me. When I travel and call home, Bruce can't wait to talk to me. But my wife has to go look for Peter and ask him to come to the phone. Things are okay, but I sense that they're not really right, and I don't have the faintest idea what to do."

This executive has been aware of this "problem" for the last three or four years. He is puzzled, but hasn't done anything about it. He is afraid that he may make things worse if he tries to improve them.

What is intriguing about this all too common situation is that the executive involved doesn't realize that it's difficult to learn to resolve the problems of private life, or that it may take time and, above all, enthusiasm and imagination to learn to identify and enjoy private life's opportunities and pleasures.

FEAR OF CONFRONTING CONFLICTS IN MARRIAGE

When working with executives in seminars, I ask them to write a list of "issues that you and your spouse do not talk about sufficiently." Each time I get the same response. After a brief pause for laughter, people settle down to write and then become quite serious. Later I ask them to write down the reasons why they do not talk enough about these issues.

The most common reasons given for avoiding discussions are fear of being rejected, facing the unknown (one never knows where such exchanges may lead), having to confront painful decisions, having to change, and showing vulnerability.

At first glance, these reasons will probably appear sensible and, perhaps, familiar. But a deeper analysis will reveal the more important reasons people are immobilized in personal relationships. They show that, for the most part, people focus on the potential negative consequences of exploring issues with their spouses without analyzing equally thoroughly the possible benefits. But, above all, they fail to mention what in my opinion are the main reasons for avoiding such exchanges. Because these exchanges are extremely rare, people don't know how to go about them. When people explain their lack of candor with each other by describing its potential catastrophic consequences, it's likely they are not accustomed to making such disclosures regularly and it is the discomfort of the exchange per se that they try to avoid.

The reasoning many people use when trying to decide whether to explore difficult issues openly often looks like this:

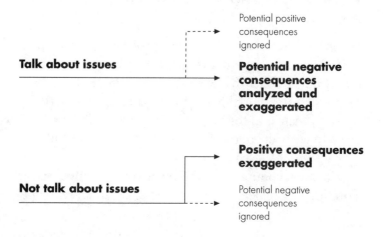

Talk about issues

Potential positive consequences ignored

Potential negative consequences analyzed and exaggerated

Not talk about issues

Positive consequences exaggerated

Potential negative consequences ignored

After making such a biased analysis, a person could reach only one conclusion: it is better not to rock the boat. But not confronting difficult issues is no solution. I am not saying, of course, that confrontation is easy or painless. It can be done, however. (I indicate how later on in this article.)

LEGITIMATE DISTRACTIONS

The persistence of problems in marital relationships is frequently due to what are seen as legitimate distractions for avoiding communication. The literature of family therapy describes the most frequent pattern. The situation that executives, particularly younger ones, find familiar, develops as follows:

A couple gets married. Natural conflicts develop in the relationship. Some of them surface and the couple deals with them in the early stages of the marriage. However, they often perceive deeper issues as too difficult to confront. Both husband and wife may find excessive work a wonderful excuse not to face these issues. Then a natural "solution" arrives in the form of a child. Now the man and woman do not need to talk about their problems; they can talk for hours on end about issues concerning the child. If one is not enough, two children are sure to give them plenty to talk about. Moreover, as children grow they begin to satisfy for each parent some of the needs the other parent fails to meet. The couple continues to postpone dealing with hidden marital conflicts.

Work and children are dangerous distractions from dealing with marital issues. They are dangerous because they are such legitimate, right, and perfect excuses. But, of the two, because they compete directly with the marriage for time and energy that may be necessary to overcome marital problems, the most dangerous distractions are children.

Family therapists often find a fear of confronting marital issues so strong that if a family comes for help with a problem child and the therapeutic intervention is effective, the parents panic. As the distraction disappears, the couple loses an excuse for avoiding confrontation of their marital issues.

'MAÑANA'

The label says it all.

You are 25 and married. You are young and starting your career. You are exploring your skills, trying to find your professional niche, trying to get on "the fast track." You are busy and decide that you will take care of your private life "mañana."

Mañana—you are 30. You have a 3-year-old child, and you have either found a good track or are still looking for one. If you are doing well, the demands of work keep increasing. If you are doing poorly, you are still struggling to find your way. You decide that you'll take care of your private life mañana.

At 35, you have made it to your first goal. You are vice president in charge of the most important single account in your firm. You relate well to your boss, who has told you that you are on the home stretch. You earn much more than the people you started out with. Yet sometimes you experience a feeling of emptiness and fear. One of the top people in your firm, who is 55, tells you, "You know, I learned all that has to be learned in this industry in the first ten years." Because that's how you feel, it scares you. But you don't know how to deal with that vague feeling of anxiety. You think that you may be hitting the midlife crisis prematurely. You decide to wait and see if this too will pass.

Mañana—you are 40 and, as happens to many men and women at this age, you want to turn toward your private life. And you decide that now is the time.

Many people in all walks of life have experienced a version of this tale. While they are making sacrifices, they keep saying to themselves that they will recapture what they are giving up. This, of course, is impossible. The experience a person misses today can't be had tomorrow. If you don't enjoy your relationship with your spouse when you are 25, the chance to do so is gone forever. If at 40 you divorce and marry someone younger, you will still be 40.

The woman (or man) who decides to invest in a career and postpone a family until she is 30 or 35 may have a wonderful experience. But raising a small child when you are 35 is not the same as doing it when you are 25. We cannot recover the relationship that we didn't have with our children when they were young. Many parents discover to their regret that they have missed their children's childhood.

People who forfeit the present risk the quality of their future private lives. As in business, you have to invest today to enjoy the returns tomorrow. The parent who tries suddenly to establish a friendship with his or her 16-year-old son or daughter after years of neglect often learns that it is too late.

Turning the Corner

Now that I've outlined the main sources of problems executives have managing their personal lives, I want to focus on potential solutions.

AVOID SAYING 'MAÑANA'

Realizing the futility of thinking that tomorrow we can recapture today and understanding how much is at stake may help executives avoid missing the present. But it is not easy to change habits of thought and behavior.

I mentioned earlier that many executives say they feel guilty about paying too little attention to their private lives. Guilt feelings generally mean a belief of not doing one's duty. As long as people think of private life more as a duty than as a pleasure and an opportunity, they are likely to find excuses to stay longer at work than they need to. On the other hand, when people stop thinking of their home life as one more chore and learn to enjoy it, they may start organizing themselves to leave work on time.

While some people show great creativity in enjoying private life, for many the time they spend with their families is unexciting. For these people their home life is blandly passive; they experience it as a spectator. Developing creative, appealing ways of being with their families is crucial for executives because it determines the force of the pull that their home lives will exert over them.

How, for instance, could the father with the two different sons, one very close to him and the other extremely distant, deal with his problem? Let me give two examples of such a case. The first shows an unproductive way of dealing with such a problem. The second is an example of a creative solution.

In the first case, the executive was sensitive and shy. His son was 12 years old and doing very well at school. He appeared to be happy, but he was also shy and seemed to have problems making friends. The executive wanted to have a closer relationship and also wanted to help his son overcome his shyness. One day he proposed that they go camping together. His son agreed, but one week before the camping trip he sprained his ankle while playing tennis. The trip was cancelled. The father waited until the following summer and again proposed a camping trip. Three weeks before the second trip his son broke his leg playing basketball.

What went wrong? It is clear that the camping trip was a bad idea. It meant moving abruptly from great distance to excessive closeness, and the child subconsciously managed to avoid it.

Another father with a similar problem dealt with it more creatively. He noticed that his 13-year-old child was studying botany at school and had a couple of new plants in his room. The father was very proud of the garden he himself tended in the backyard. One day he told his son in passing, "You know, I'm not using all the space in the back. If you want to plant anything, feel free." The son planted melons, and soon he was coming to his father for advice.

In the second case, both the "solution" and the process were right. The father first paid attention to his son's growing interest in plants. Second, he approached his son gently suggesting "in passing," that he plant something; instead of invading his son's territory, the father invited him into his own. Finally, it was their common interest and gradually increasing physical proximity that brought father and child together. It was an elegant solution to a complex problem.

DEAL WITH CONFLICTS

Paradoxically, before a couple can address its problems, both people have to establish first that the marriage can be improved. People need hope, and this they can gain by determining what does work and what is good in the relationship. When I ask people to list issues that they are not discussing with their spouses, often their lists include only problems: "our disagreements about raising the children"; "the ways in which he or she disappointed or hurt me"; "what we have lost."

But people will only work to solve conflicts if they believe the relationship can be improved and if the atmosphere is right for them to do the necessary work.

Before starting to address problems, people should talk about the opposite side of the coin, about what is good and works well in their marriage—to rephrase the list above: "our agreements on raising the children"; "the ways in which I am proud of you"; "how you have helped me"; "what we have created"—then they'll know that it is worthwhile fighting to improve the relationship and that they have the resources to deal with existing problems. Talking about what is good can help them see not only the potential catastrophic consequences of a dialogue but also the benefits.

Emphasizing the positive can also create an atmosphere of warmth and trust that can make talking about conflicts less threatening.

Dealing with conflict itself requires that people learn two fundamental skills. The first is, as a matter of everyday practice, continuing a dialogue instead of letting emotions accumulate and eventually explode. This means learning to give not only negative but also positive feedback. Many people, particularly men, have as much trouble expressing positive as they do negative feelings.[2]

The second skill is dealing with persistent and deeper conflicts. In most cases, couples who find it exceedingly difficult to handle conflicts have a long history of poor communication marked by sporadic and usually unsuccessful attempts to cope with important issues. As a consequence, a couple with such a track record associates discussing conflicts openly with emotional explosions, hurt egos, and catastrophes. The couple believes "once burned, twice shy."

Here is an example of what such a couple fears when extreme feelings in one or both of the parties necessitate a "conversation." Under conditions of heightened emotion, such a conversation promptly turns into reciprocal blaming, explosion, and withdrawal. In this case, a couple was discussing their children. The exchange started gently, but then the wife told the husband that he was being too rough with 11-year-old Paul, who was having problems in school.

The dialogue, that I witnessed, went something like this:

"You're too rough with him. He's scared of you."

"Somebody has to do the disciplining around here and you don't do it!"

"Okay, but you don't need to be so brutal."

"I am not brutal. The children see me as brutal because you don't confront them at all and leave that job to me. You tell them 'wait until your father comes home!' "

"That doesn't justify your behavior."

"You want me to discipline the children when I come home from the office completely exhausted. How do you expect me to behave?"

"You see, I can't talk with you. You get all upset and start blaming it all on me! . . ."

In this conversation the blaming game is in full bloom. But how can a couple avoid this? One way is to keep track of how the conversation is going and at the first sign of excessive emotional tension, to stop to recover some equanimity and some warmth.

But even stopping to examine what is going on in the conversation to make sure things don't go wrong can become part of the blaming game—"you interrupt me all the time," "you never listen,"—so people have to learn how to talk constructively.

This is no easy feat. But learning how to build a bridge, create a company, or sell something isn't easy either, and people do learn.

BECOME AUTHENTIC

For some people, having fun in a relationship comes naturally. For others, whose lives have become routine, reawakening a sense of excitement and pleasure in a relationship may be difficult. The easy solution is, of course, to go after the greener grass on the other side of the fence. But in most cases the price people pay for straying is very high.

Of course, not all relationships can be revitalized or launched anew. Some may be beyond hope, and the issue a couple faces is how to end it without undue pain and destruction and have what therapists refer to as a "creative divorce." But my contact with executives makes me think that many have relationships that are satisfactory but could be vastly improved.

How can a marriage be revitalized? To build a relationship that satisfies both partners' needs and allows them to have fun, each has to be able to clearly ask for what he or she needs or would enjoy. Some people feel, however, that they shouldn't need to ask, that their partners should know them well enough to realize or sense what they need. This can happen only when a couple is so transparent that they never lie to each other with either words or behavior.

Some people say that they are "afraid of rejection." And by using the word "rejection" they indicate how little clarity and honesty they achieve in their communication. When a person says he or she fears rejection, he or she conveys the idea that the other may reject what is being offered. But, in most cases, when people talk about fear of rejection, what they fear is not that their love will be spurned but that they will not be loved in return. In truth, fear of rejection is a fear that the other will not give us what we need or want. When people fear they won't get what they need and do not ask honestly for it because of that fear, indeed they end up not getting it.

If people are to have true pleasure in relationships, they need to learn both to get rid of excessive fears and unconscious fantasies and to be authentic. A transparent person shows his or her needs and problems—and also shows joy and pleasure. Only when two people own up to their deepest feelings can the true issues between them arise, namely, the extent to which they are deeply and naturally compatible or the extent to which their mutual attraction can motivate them to adapt to each other. The courage to be transparent does not come easily, however. Fears can be very deep. As Erik Erikson has said, hope and trust are basic virtues that people have to develop. This requires intelligent risk taking, courage, and luck.

When behavior is authentic, both partners can learn what the other person needs, how he or she feels, what he or she truly enjoys, and what hurts. The transparency of one partner tends to evoke transparency in the other. And most important, being able to see each other clearly, people learn to trust each other.

How many married people really trust the messages of pleasure that their partner expresses when making love? My guess is that those who really trust their partners are the same ones who, during those times, never lie with words or acts. And what will happen to trust if we don't trust each other in our most intimate moments?

But sometimes being authentic cannot guarantee getting what we need. Then it is necessary to talk. If a couple is transparent on a daily basis, they will find that talk comes easily; what makes communication problematic is the unwillingness to be candid. When people are ready to be candid, communication may involve pain but it is not in itself difficult.

Authentic behavior and clear communication are, together with imagination and playfulness, the doors to pleasure in relationships.

Making It Work

How can executives begin to enhance the quality of their home lives? The first step is to abandon the assumption that having a good private life is easy or that they can easily acquire the necessary skills. Most people find it difficult.

The second step is to abandon the equally incorrect assumption that personal relationships are too complex and difficult to handle and, therefore, people shouldn't even try. In their private lives as in their professional lives, executives need to establish clear, concrete, and achievable goals and to monitor their achievement.

Private goals are often implicit or impossibly vague, and many are extremely unrealistic. People need to ask themselves what they want their marital relationships to be, or what they would like their relationship with a child to be, and what their self-development goals are. If the answers to these questions are general statements—"I want a good relationship with my husband" or "I want to be friends with my children"—it is necessary to ask, "What does that mean?"

To say, "I want to spend more time alone with my husband" is not enough. To specify that "Every week I will make sure that I spend at least two hours alone with him doing something that we both enjoy" is much more likely to work. To say, "I want to have a better relationship with my son" is too vague. To say, "I will first stop and think about what is causing problems between us, and then figure out what we may enjoy doing together" is a more logical way to proceed.

In talking with executives about these kinds of issues, I suggest they select one or two improvement projects at home. These may be taking better care of their health or of their self-development or improving their relationships with their wife, children, or friends. I recommend that the projects have the following characteristics: to begin with they should be *modest,* not revolutionary; they should yield results that are *measurable* so that the executive can notice a difference, and *pleasurable* so that the executive will enjoy the outcome; and, finally, they should *involve another person* who will help the executive persist.

I caution readers not to attempt to address the most difficult issues at the beginning. Because nothing succeeds like success, you should attempt to improve "small" things first, thereby learning new skills and signaling clearly an intention to improve relationships. The results are often surprising.

And finally, I encourage you to suspend your skepticism, although this can be difficult. Recently I talked with a couple who had tried this approach, and the wife assured me that "It has really worked." Small changes can make a significant difference for those who, lacking insurmountable problems, sense that something is missing at home and want to improve the quality of their private lives.

It's Never Too Late

Many people tend to believe that, late in life, it is too difficult to change. Today, adult development research shows that people have a much greater capacity to change and learn through life than was assumed. Some people argue that personal skills are fully intuitive and either you have them or you don't. But the main component in dealing with many private life issues is interpersonal sensitivity, and my experience is that people have much more sensitivity than they give themselves credit for. I consistently find that what on the surface looks like insensitivity hides, in reality, a deep hypersensitivity. Under the right conditions, people can uncover their hypersensitivity, transform it into sensitivity, and put it to work. With very little prodding, their hope can be rekindled.

What It's All About

I GET HOME AROUND SIX-THIRTY, seven at night. After dinner with the family I spend a minimum of two and a half hours each night going over the mail and dictating. I should have a secretary at home just to handle the mail that comes there. I'm not talking about bills and personal notes, I'm talking about business mail only. Although I don't go to the office on Saturday or Sunday, I do have mail brought out to my home for the weekend. I dictate on Saturday and Sunday. When I do this on holidays, like Christmas, New Year's, and Thanksgiving, I have to sneak a little bit, so the family doesn't know what I'm doing.

Ward Quaal
Television & radio executive

From Studs Terkel, Working (New York: Pantheon Books), 1974. With permission from the publisher.

Notes

1. For a discussion of research on this subject, see my article, coauthored with Paul A. Lee Evans, "Must Success Cost So Much?" HBR, March–April 1980, p. 137. (Chapter 2 of this book)

2. See my article, "Executives as Human Beings," HBR, November–December 1972, p. 62.

Originally published in March–April 1983
Reprint 83204

Management Women and the New Facts of Life

FELICE N. SCHWARTZ

Executive Summary

WOMEN MANAGERS COST MORE to employ than men. Turnover is higher, and they are more apt to plateau or to interrupt their careers. So companies are more likely to lose the money they invest in developing women managers. But, because population growth is down, women in business have moved from a buyer's to a seller's market.

The disparity in cost has two causes: maternity and tradition. Many women take maternity leave, and some find it difficult to return to work on schedule. But even an extended maternity leave is a small portion of a whole career. The real cost differential—lost investment in women—is a result of the clash between male and female expectations.

Management women range from those whose careers come first—often to the exclusion of family—to those who try to balance career and family equally. The male corporation dislikes both extremes. The first seems too masculine, the second seems lacking in commitment. Yet both are badly needed.

Smart, competitive, *career-primary women* are effective managers and serve as beacons for the younger women companies need. *Career-and-family women,* on the other hand, are willing to trade ambition for the flexibility to raise their families. This willingness to forgo advancement but still give their best can greatly upgrade middle management.

Opportunity, flexibility, and family support are the keys to retaining the best women and eliminating the extra cost of employing them. Opportunity means judging and promoting ambitious women on the same terms as men. Flexibility means allowing women to share jobs or work part-time while their children are young. Family suppport means, principally, child care.

THE COST OF EMPLOYING WOMEN in management is greater than the cost of employing men. This is a jarring statement, partly because it is true, but mostly because it is something people are reluctant to talk about. A new study by one multinational corporation shows that the rate of turnover in management positions is 2 ½ times higher among top-performing women than it is among men. A large producer of consumer goods reports that one half of the women who take maternity leave return to their jobs late or not at all. And we know that women also have a greater tendency to plateau or to interrupt their careers in ways that limit their growth and development. But we have become so sensitive to charges of sexism and so afraid of confrontation, even litigation, that we rarely say what we know to be true. Unfortunately, our bottled-up awareness leaks out in misleading metaphors ("glass ceiling" is one notable example), veiled hostility, lowered expectations, distrust, and reluctant adherence to Equal Employment Opportunity requirements.

Career interruptions, plateauing, and turnover are expensive. The money corporations invest in recruitment, training, and development is less likely to produce top executives among women than among men, and the invaluable company experience that developing executives acquire at every level as they move up through management ranks is more often lost.

The studies just mentioned are only the first of many, I'm quite sure. Demographic realities are going to force corporations all across the country to analyze the cost of employing women in managerial positions, and what they will discover is that women cost more.

But here is another startling truth: The greater cost of employing women is not a function of inescapable gender differences. Women *are* different from men, but what increases their cost to the corporation is principally the clash of their perceptions, attitudes, and behavior with those of men, which is to say, with the policies and practices of male-led corporations.

It is terribly important that employers draw the right conclusions from the studies now being done. The studies will be useless—or worse, harmful—if all they teach us is that women are expensive to employ. What we need to learn is how to reduce that expense, how to stop throwing away the investments we make in talented women, how to become more responsive to the needs of the women that corporations *must* employ if they are to have the best and the brightest of all those now entering the work force.

The gender differences relevant to business fall into two categories: those related to maternity and those related to the differing traditions and expectations of the sexes. Maternity is biological rather than cultural. We can't alter it, but we can dramatically reduce its impact on the workplace and in many cases eliminate its negative effect on employee development. We can accomplish this by addressing the second set of differences, those between male and female socialization. Today, these differences exaggerate the real costs of maternity and can turn a relatively slight disruption in work schedule into a serious business problem and a career derailment for individual women. If we are to overcome the cost differential between male and female employees, we need to address the issues that arise when female socialization meets the male corporate culture and masculine rules of career development—issues of behavior and style, of expectation, of stereotypes and preconceptions, of sexual tension and harassment, of female mentoring, lateral mobility, relocation, compensation, and early identification of top performers.

Two facts matter to business: only women have babies and only men make rules.

T HE ONE IMMUTABLE, enduring difference between men and women is maternity. Maternity is not simply childbirth but a continuum that begins with an awareness of the ticking of the biological clock, proceeds to the anticipation of motherhood, includes pregnancy, childbirth, physical recuperation, psychological adjustment, and continues on to nursing, bonding, and child rearing. Not all women choose to become mothers, of course, and among those who do, the process varies from case to case depending on the health of the mother and baby, the values of the parents, and the availability, cost, and quality of child care.

In past centuries, the biological fact of maternity shaped the traditional roles of the sexes. Women performed the home-centered functions that related to the bearing and nurturing of children. Men did the work that required great physical strength. Over time, however, family size contracted, the community assumed greater responsibility for the care and education of children, packaged foods and household technology reduced the work load in the home, and technology eliminated much of the need for muscle power at the workplace. Today in the developed world, the only role still uniquely gender related is childbearing. Yet men and women are still socialized to perform their traditional roles.

Men and women may or may not have some innate psychological disposition toward these traditional roles—men to be aggressive, competitive, self-reliant, risk taking; women to be supportive, nurturing, intuitive, sensitive, communicative—but certainly both men and women are capable of the full range of behavior. Indeed, the male and female roles have already begun to expand and merge. In the decades ahead, as the socialization of boys and girls and the experience and expectations of young men and women grow steadily more androgynous, the differences in workplace behavior will

Women who compete like men are considered unfeminine. Women who emphasize family are considered uncommitted.

continue to fade. At the moment, however, we are still plagued by disparities in perception and behavior that make the integration of men and women in the workplace unnecessarily difficult and expensive.

Let me illustrate with a few broadbrush generalizations. Of course, these are only stereotypes, but I think they help to exemplify the kinds of preconceptions that can muddy the corporate waters.

Men continue to perceive women as the rearers of their children, so they find it understandable, indeed appropriate, that women should renounce their careers to raise families. Edmund Pratt, CEO of Pfizer, once asked me in all sincerity, "Why would any woman choose to be a chief financial officer rather than a full-time mother?" By condoning and taking pleasure in women's traditional behavior, men reinforce it. Not only do they see parenting as fundamentally female, they see a career as fundamentally male—either an unbroken series of promotions and advancements toward CEOdom or stagnation and disappointment. This attitude serves to legitimize a woman's choice to extend maternity leave and even, for those who can afford it, to leave employment altogether for several years. By the same token, men who might want to take a leave after the birth of a child know that management will see such behavior as a lack of career commitment, even when company policy permits parental leave for men.

Women also bring counterproductive expectations and perceptions to the workplace. Ironically, although the feminist movement was an expression of women's quest for freedom from their home-based lives, most women were remarkably free already. They had many responsibilities, but they were autonomous and could be entrepreneurial in how and when they carried them out.

And once their children grew up and left home, they were essentially free to do what they wanted with their lives. Women's traditional role also included freedom from responsibility for the financial support of their families. Many of us were socialized from girlhood to expect our husbands to take care of us, while our brothers were socialized from an equally early age to complete their educations, pursue careers, climb the ladder of success, and provide dependable financial support for their families. To the extent that this tradition of freedom lingers subliminally, women tend to bring to their employment a sense that they can choose to change jobs or careers at will, take time off, or reduce their hours.

Finally, women's traditional role encouraged particular attention to the quality and substance of what they did, specifically to the physical, psychological, and intellectual development of their children. This traditional focus may explain women's continuing tendency to search for more than monetary reward—intrinsic significance, social importance, meaning—in what they do. This too makes them more likely than men to leave the corporation in search of other values.

The misleading metaphor of the glass ceiling suggests an invisible barrier constructed by corporate leaders to impede the upward mobility of women beyond the middle levels. A more appropriate metaphor, I believe, is the kind of cross-sectional diagram used in geology. The barriers to women's leadership occur when potentially counterproductive layers of influence on women— maternity, tradition, socialization—meet management strata pervaded by the largely unconscious preconceptions, stereotypes, and expectations of men. Such interfaces do not exist for men and tend to be impermeable for women.

One result of these gender differences has been to convince some executives that women are simply not suited to top management. Other executives feel help-less. If they see even a few of their valued female

With too few men to go around, women have moved from a buyer's to a seller's market.

employees fail to return to work from maternity leave on schedule or see one of their most promising women plateau in her career after the birth of a child, they begin to

fear there is nothing they can do to infuse women with new energy and enthusiasm and persuade them to stay. At the same time, they know there is nothing they can do to stem the tide of women into management ranks.

Another result is to place every working woman on a continuum that runs from total dedication to career at one end to a balance between career and family at the other. What women discover is that the male corporate culture sees both extremes as unacceptable. Women who want the flexibility to balance their families and their careers are not adequately committed to the organiza-tion. Women who perform as aggressively and competi-tively as men are abrasive and unfeminine. But the fact is, business needs all the talented women it can get. Moreover, as I will explain, the women I call career-primary and those I call career-and-family each have par-ticular value to the corporation.

W OMEN IN THE CORPORATION are about to move from a buyer's to a seller's market. The sudden, startling recognition that 80% of new entrants in the work force over the next decade will be women, minorities, and immigrants has stimulated a mushrooming incentive to "value diversity."

Women are no longer simply an enticing pool of occasional creative talent, a thorn in the side of the EEO officer, or a source of frustration to corporate leaders truly puzzled by the slowness of their upward trickle into executive positions. A real demographic change is taking place. The era of sudden population growth of the 1950s and 1960s is over. The birth rate has dropped about 40%, from a high of 25.3 live births per 1,000 population in 1957, at the peak of the baby boom, to a stable low of a little more than 15 per 1,000 over the last 16 years, and there is no indication of a return to a higher rate. The tidal wave of baby boomers that swelled the recruitment pool to overflowing seems to have been a one-time phenomenon. For 20 years, employers had the pick of a very large crop and were able to choose males almost exclusively for the executive track. But if future population remains fairly stable while the economy continues to expand, and if the new information society simultaneously creates a greater need for creative, educated managers, then the gap between supply and demand will grow dramatically and, with it, the competition for managerial talent.

The decrease in numbers has even greater implications if we look at the traditional source of corporate recruitment for leadership positions—white males from the top 10% of the country's best universities. Over the past decade, the increase in the number of women graduating from leading universities has been much greater than the increase in the total number of graduates, and these women are well represented in the top 10% of their classes.

The trend extends into business and professional programs as well. In the old days, virtually all MBAs were male. I remember addressing a meeting at the Harvard Business School as recently as the mid-1970s and looking out at a sea of exclusively male faces. Today, about 25% of that audience would be women. The pool of male MBAs from which corporations have traditionally drawn their leaders has shrunk significantly.

Of course, this reduction does not have to mean a shortage of talent. The top 10% is at least as smart as it always was—smarter, probably, since it's now drawn from a broader segment of the population. But it now consists increasingly of women. Companies that are determined to recruit the same number of men as before will have to dig much deeper into the male pool, while their competitors will have the opportunity to pick the best people from both the male and female graduates.

UNDER THESE CIRCUMSTANCES, there is no question that the management ranks of business will include increasing numbers of women. There remains, however, the question of how these women will succeed—how long they will stay, how high they will climb, how completely they will fulfill their promise and potential, and what kind of return the corporation will realize on its investment in their training and development.

There is ample business reason for finding ways to make sure that as many of these women as possible will succeed. The first step in this process is to recognize that women are not all alike. Like men, they are individuals with differing talents, priorities, and motivations. For the sake of simplicity, let me focus on the two women I referred to earlier, on what I call the career-primary woman and the career-and-family woman.

Like many men, some women put their careers first. They are ready to make the same trade-offs traditionally made by the men who seek leadership positions. They make a career decision to put in extra hours, to make sacrifices in their personal lives, to make the most of every opportunity for professional development. For women, of course, this decision also requires that they remain single or at least childless or, if they do have children, that they be satisfied to have others raise them. Some 90% of executive men but only 35% of executive women have children by the age of 40. The *automatic* association of all women with babies is clearly unjustified.

It is absurd to put a woman down for having the very qualities that would send a man to the top.

The secret to dealing with such women is to recognize them early, accept them, and clear artificial barriers from their path to the top. After all, the best of these women are among the best managerial talent you will ever see. And career-primary women have another important value to the company that men and other women lack. They can act as role models and mentors to younger women who put their careers first. Since upwardly mobile career-primary women still have few role models to motivate and inspire them, a company with women in its top echelon has a significant advantage in the competition for executive talent.

Men at the top of the organization—most of them over 55, with wives who tend to be traditional—often find career women "masculine" and difficult to accept as colleagues. Such men miss the point, which is not that these women are just like men but that they are just like the *best* men in the organization. And there is such a shortage of the best people that gender cannot be allowed to matter. It is clearly counterproductive to disparage in a woman with executive talent the very qualities that are most critical to the business and that might carry a man to the CEO's office.

Clearing a path to the top for career-primary women has four requirements:

1. Identify them early.

2. Give them the same opportunity you give to talented men to grow and develop and contribute to company profitability. Give them client and customer responsibility. Expect them to travel and relocate, to make the same commitment to the company as men aspiring to leadership positions.

3. Accept them as valued members of your management team. Include them in every kind of communication. Listen to them.

4. Recognize that the business environment is more difficult and stressful for them than for their male peers. They are always a minority, often the only woman. The male perception of talented, ambitious women is at best ambivalent, a mixture of admiration, resentment, confusion, competitiveness, attraction, skepticism, anxiety, pride, and animosity. Women can never feel secure about how they should dress and act, whether they should speak out or grin and bear it when they encounter discrimination, stereotyping, sexual harassment, and paternalism. Social interaction and travel with male colleagues and with male clients can be charged. As they move up, the normal increase in pressure and responsibil-

ity is compounded for women because they are women.

Stereotypical language and sexist day-to-day behavior do take their toll on women's career development. Few male executives realize how common it is to call women by their first names while men in the same group are greeted with surnames, how frequently female executives are assumed by men to be secretaries, how often women are excluded from all-male social events where business is being transacted. With notable exceptions, men are still generally more comfortable with other men, and as a result women miss many of the career and business opportunities that arise over lunch, on the golf course, or in the locker room.

T HE MAJORITY OF WOMEN, however, are what I call career-and-family women, women who want to pursue serious careers while participating actively in the rearing of children. These women are a precious resource that has yet to be mined. Many of them are talented and creative. Most of them are willing to trade some career growth and compensation for freedom from the constant pressure to work long hours and weekends.

Most companies today are ambivalent at best about the career-and-family women in their management ranks. They would prefer that all employees were willing to give their all to the company. They believe it is in their best interests for all managers to compete for the top positions so the company will have the largest possible pool from which to draw its leaders.

"If you have both talent and motivation," many employers seem to say, "we want to move you up. If you haven't got that motivation, if you want less pressure and greater flexibility, then you can leave and make room for a new generation." These companies lose on two counts. First, they fail to amortize the investment they made in the early training and experience of management women who find themselves committed to family as well as to career. Second, they fail to recognize what these women could do for their middle management.

A policy that forces women to choose between family and career cuts hugely into profits and competitive advantage.

The ranks of middle managers are filled with people on their way up and people who have stalled. Many of them have simply reached their limits, achieved career growth commensurate with or exceeding their capabilities, and they cause problems because their performance is mediocre, but they still want to move ahead. The career-and-family woman is willing to trade off the pressures and demands that go with promotion for the freedom to spend more time with her children. She's very smart, she's talented, she's committed to her career, and she's satisfied to stay at the middle level, at least during the early child-rearing years. Compare her with some of the people you have there now.

Consider a typical example, a woman who decides in college on a business career and enters management at age 22. For nine years, the company invests in her career as she gains experience and skills and steadily improves her performance. But at 31, just as the investment begins to pay off in earnest, she decides to have a baby. Can the company afford to let her go home, take another job, or go into business for herself? The common perception now is yes, the corporation can afford to lose her unless, after six or eight weeks or even three months of disability and maternity leave, she returns to work on a full-time schedule with the same vigor, commitment, and ambition that she showed before.

But what if she doesn't? What if she wants or needs to go on leave for six months or a year or, heaven forbid, five years? In this worst-case scenario, she works full-time from age 22 to 31 and from 36 to 65—a total of 38 years as opposed to the typical male's 43 years. That's not a huge difference. Moreover, my typical example is willing to work part-time while her children are young, if only her employer will give her the opportunity. There are two rewards for companies responsive to this need: higher retention of their best people and greatly improved performance and satisfaction in their middle management.

The high-performing career-and-family woman can be a major player in your company. She can give you a significant business advantage as the competition for able people escalates. Sometimes too, if you can hold on to her, she will switch gears in mid-life and re-enter the competition for the top. The price you must pay to retain these women is threefold: you must plan for and manage maternity, you must provide the flexibility that will allow them to be maximally productive, and you must take an active role in helping to make family supports and high-quality, affordable child care available to all women.

THE KEY TO MANAGING MATERNITY is to recognize the value of high-performing women and the urgent need to retain them and keep them productive. The first step must be a genuine partnership between the woman and her boss. I know this partnership can seem difficult to forge. One of my own senior executives came to me recently to discuss plans for her maternity leave and

subsequent return to work. She knew she wanted to
come back. I wanted to make certain that she would.
Still, we had a somewhat awkward conversation, because
I knew that no woman can predict with certainty when
she will be able to return to work or under what conditions. Physical problems can lengthen her leave. So can a
demanding infant, a difficult family or personal adjustment, or problems with child care.

I still don't know when this valuable executive will be
back on the job full-time, and her absence creates some
genuine problems for our organization. But I do know
that I can't simply replace her years of experience with a
new recruit. Since our conversation, I also know that she
wants to come back, and that she *will* come back—part-
time at first—unless I make it impossible for her by, for
example, setting an arbitrary date for her full-time return
or resignation. In turn, she knows that the organization
wants and needs her and, more to the point, that it will
be responsive to her needs in terms of working hours and
child-care arrangements.

In having this kind of conversation it's important to
ask concrete questions that will help to move the discussion from uncertainty and anxiety to some level of predictability. Questions can touch on everything from family income and energy level to child care arrangements
and career commitment. Of course you want your star
manager to return to work as soon as possible, but you
want her to return permanently and productively. Her
downtime on the job is a drain on her energies and a
waste of your money.

For all the women who want to combine career
and family—the women who want to participate actively

in the rearing of their children and who also want to pursue their careers seriously—the key to retention is to provide the flexibility and family supports they need in order to function effectively.

Time spent in the office increases productivity if it is time well spent, but the fact that most women continue to take the primary responsibility for child care is a cause of distraction, diversion, anxiety, and absenteeism—to say nothing of the persistent guilt experienced by all working mothers. A great many women, perhaps most of all women who have always performed at the highest levels, are also frustrated by a sense that while their children are babies they cannot function at their best either at home or at work.

In its simplest form, flexibility is the freedom to take time off—a couple of hours, a day, a week—or to do some work at home and some at the office, an arrangement that communication technology makes increasingly feasible. At the complex end of the spectrum are alternative work schedules that permit the woman to work less than full-time and her employer to reap the benefits of her experience and, with careful planning, the top level of her abilities.

Part-time employment is the single greatest inducement to getting women back on the job expeditiously and the provision women themselves most desire. A part-time return to work enables them to maintain responsibility for critical aspects of their jobs, keeps them in touch with the changes constantly occurring at the workplace and in the job itself, reduces stress and fatigue, often eliminates the need for paid maternity leave by permitting a return to the office as soon as disability leave is over, and, not least, can greatly enhance company loyalty. The part-time solution works particularly well when a work load can be reduced for one individual in a department or when a full-time job can be broken down by skill levels and apportioned to two individuals at different levels of skill and pay.

I believe, however, that shared employment is the most promising and will be the most widespread form of flexible scheduling in the future. It is feasible at every level of the corporation except at the pinnacle, for both the short and the long term. It involves two people taking responsibility for one job.

Two red lights flash on as soon as most executives hear the words "job sharing": continuity and client-customer contact. The answer to the continuity question is to place responsibility entirely on the two individuals sharing the job to discuss everything that transpires— thoroughly, daily, and on their own time. The answer to the problem of client-customer contact is yes, job sharing requires reeducation and a period of adjustment. But as both client and supervisor will quickly come to appreciate, two contacts means that the customer has continuous access to the company's representative, without interruptions for vacation, travel, or sick leave. The two people holding the job can simply cover for each other, and the uninterrupted, full-time coverage they provide together can be a stipulation of their arrangement.

Flexibility is costly in numerous ways. It requires more supervisory time to coordinate and manage, more office space, and somewhat greater benefits costs (though these can be contained with flexible benefits plans, prorated benefits, and, in two-paycheck families, elimination of duplicate benefits). But the advantages of reduced turnover and the greater productivity that results from higher energy levels and greater focus can outweigh the costs.

A few hints:

- Provide flexibility selectively. I'm not suggesting private arrangements subject to the suspicion of favoritism but rather a policy that makes flexible work schedules available only to high performers.

- Make it clear that in most instances (but not all) the rates of advancement and pay will be appropriately lower for those who take time off or who work part-time than for those who work full-time. Most career-and-family women are entirely willing to make that trade-off.

- Discuss costs as well as benefits. Be willing to risk accusations of bias. Insist, for example, that half time is half of whatever time it takes to do the job, not merely half of 35 or 40 hours.

The woman who is eager to get home to her child has a powerful incentive to use her time effectively at the office and to carry with her reading and other work that can be done at home. The talented professional who wants to have it all can be a high performer by carefully ordering her priorities and by focusing on objectives rather than on the legendary 15-hour day. By the time professional women have their first babies—at an average age of 31—they have already had nine years to work long hours at a desk, to travel, and to relocate. In the case of high performers, the need for flexibility coincides with what has gradually become the goal-oriented nature of responsibility.

F AMILY SUPPORTS—in addition to maternity leave and flexibility—include the provision of parental leave for men, support for two-career and single-parent families during relocation, and flexible benefits. But the primary ingredient is child care. The capacity of working mothers to function effectively and without interruption depends on the availability of good, affordable child care. Now that women make up almost half the work force and the growing percentage of managers, the decision to become involved in the personal lives of employees is no longer a philosophical question but a practical one. To make matters worse, the quality of child care has almost no relation to technology, inventiveness, or profitability but is more or less a pure function of the quality of child care personnel and the ratio of adults to children. These costs are irreducible. Only by joining hands with government and the public sector can corporations hope to create the vast quantity and variety of child care that their employees need.

Until quite recently, the response of corporations to women has been largely symbolic and cosmetic, motivated in large part by the will to avoid litigation and legal penalties. In some cases, companies were also moved by a genuine sense of fairness and a vague discomfort and frustration at the absence of women above the middle of the corporate pyramid. The actions they took were mostly quick, easy, and highly visible—child care information services, a three-month parental leave available to men as well as women, a woman appointed to the board of directors.

When I first began to discuss these issues 26 years ago, I was sometimes able to get an appointment with the assistant to the assistant in personnel, but it was only a courtesy. Over the past decade, I have met with the CEOs of many large corporations, and I've watched them become involved with ideas they had never previously thought much about. Until recently, however, the shelf life of that enhanced awareness was always short. Given pressing, short-term concerns, women were not a front-burner issue. In the past few months, I have seen yet another change. Some CEOs and top management groups now take the initiative. They call and ask us to show them how to shift gears from a responsive to a proactive approach to recruiting, developing, and retaining women.

Incredibly, very few companies have ever studied the costs and statistics of maternity leave.

I think this change is more probably a response to business needs—to concern for the quality of future profits and managerial talent—than to uneasiness about legal requirements, sympathy with the demands of women and minorities, or the desire to do what is right and fair. The nature of such business motivation varies. Some companies want to move women to higher positions as role models for those below them and as beacons for talented young recruits. Some want to achieve a favorable image with employees, customers, clients, and stockholders. These are all legitimate motives. But I think the companies that stand to gain most are motivated as well by a desire to capture competitive advantage in an era when talent and competence will be in increasingly short supply. These companies are now ready to stop being defensive about their experience with women and to ask incisive questions without preconceptions.

Even so, incredibly, I don't know of more than one or two companies that have looked into their own records

to study the absolutely critical issue of maternity leave—
how many women took it, when and whether they
returned, and how this behavior correlated with their
rank, tenure, age, and performance. The unique draw-
back to the employment of women is the physical reality
of maternity and the particular socializing influence
maternity has had. Yet to make women equal to men in
the workplace we have chosen on the whole not to discuss this single most significant difference between
them. Unless we do, we cannot evaluate the cost of
recruiting, developing, and moving women up.

Now that interest is replacing indifference, there are
four steps every company can take to examine its own
experience with women:

1. Gather quantitative data on the company's experience with management-level women regarding
   turnover rates, occurrence of and return from maternity leave, and organizational level attained in relation to tenure and performance.

2. Correlate this data with factors such as age, marital
   status, and presence and age of children, and
   attempt to identify and analyze why women respond
   the way they do.

3. Gather qualitative data on the experience of women
   in your company and on how women are perceived
   by both sexes.

4. Conduct a cost-benefit analysis of the return on your
   investment in high-performing women. Factor in the
   cost to the company of women's negative reactions
   to negative experience, as well as the probable cost of
   corrective measures and policies. If women's value to
   your company is greater than the cost to recruit,

train, and develop them—and of course I believe it will be—then you will want to do everything you can to retain them.

W E H A V E C O M E a tremendous distance since the days when the prevailing male wisdom saw women as lacking the kind of intelligence that would allow them to succeed in business. For decades, even women themselves have harbored an unspoken belief that they couldn't make it because they couldn't be just like men, and nothing else would do. But now that women have shown themselves the equal of men in every area of organizational activity, now that they have demonstrated that they can be stars in every field of endeavor, now we can all venture to examine the fact that women and men are different.

On balance, employing women is more costly than employing men. Women can acknowledge this fact today because they know that their value to employers exceeds the additional cost and because they know that changing attitudes can reduce the additional cost dramatically. Women in management are no longer an idiosyncrasy of the arts and education. They

Wouldn't we all be better off with men in the office and women in the home? The answer is emphatically no.

have always matched men in natural ability. Within a very few years, they will equal men in numbers as well in every area of economic activity.

The demographic motivation to recruit and develop women is compelling. But an older question remains: Is society better for the change? Women's exit from the home and entry into the work force has certainly created problems—an urgent need for good, affordable child care; troubling questions about the kind of parenting children need; the costs and difficulties of diversity in the workplace; the stress and fatigue of combining work and family responsibilities. Wouldn't we all be happier if we could turn back the clock to an age when men were in the workplace and women in the home, when male and female roles were clearly differentiated and complementary?

Nostalgia, anxiety, and discouragement will urge many to say yes, but my answer is emphatically no. Two fundamental benefits that were unattainable in the past are now within our reach. For the individual, freedom of choice—in this case the freedom to choose career, family, or a combination of the two. For the corporation, access to the most gifted individuals in the country. These benefits are neither self-indulgent nor insubstantial. Freedom of choice and self-realization are too deeply American to be cast aside for some wistful vision of the past. And access to our most talented human resources is not a luxury in this age of explosive international competition but rather the barest minimum that prudence and national self-preservation require.

Originally published in January–February 1989
Reprint 89110

What Do Men Want?

MICHAEL S. KIMMEL

Executive Summary

WHILE FREUD and countless other social commentators
of the past wrung their hands at the "mysterious" needs
of women, they never questioned what men wanted,
especially in the realm of work. After all, a man's profession and his ability to bring home a paycheck have traditionally defined who that man was. And given that most
American men grew up believing in the conventional
symbols of manhood—wealth, power, status—there are
still clear emotional and financial costs involved in making other choices.

Yet unlike the man in the gray flannel suit of the
1950s or the fast-tracker of the 1970s and 1980s,
today's organization man faces an economy in which
corporations are laying off thousands of employees. And
though many wives of male chief executives still stay at

home, spouses of most other men now work. These two trends are forcing men to redefine themselves.

A new organization man has indeed emerged, one who wants to be an involved father with no loss of income, prestige, and corporate support—and no diminished sense of manhood. But since many companies still deem dedication to career the sole marker of professional success, this new man may believe he has to hide his participation at home. Instead of taking advantage of his company's parental leave policies, for instance, he's likely to use sick days to watch over a new baby.

Not surprisingly, the compromises made by the new organization man bear a striking resemblance to those of the new organization women. And just as many senior managers now recognize that they'll lose their most ambitious women if they don't develop strategies to accommodate family needs, corporations may also lose their best and brightest men if they don't address the needs of the 1990s man.

F REUD'S FAMOUS CRY of resignation—"Women, what do they want?"—has been a feminist touchstone for nearly a century. By contrast, the good doctor and countless other social commentators always assumed they knew what men wanted, especially in the realm of work. After all, a man's profession and his ability to bring home a paycheck have traditionally defined who that man was. With wives to manage the domestic scene, working men of the past had little reason to question a system designed by and for them.

But unlike the man in the gray flannel suit of the 1950s or the fast-tracker of the 1970s and 1980s, today's organization man faces a contracting economy in which corporations are restructuring, downsizing, and laying off thousands of employees. Though many wives of male chief executives still stay at home, spouses of most other men now work. These two trends—the recent economic downturn and women's entry into the workplace—are forcing men to redefine themselves. In order to do so, men of the 1990s must reevaluate what it means to be a success, both on the job and in the home.

Not all men want the same thing, of course. Some still resist efforts to change the old rules for masculine behavior. But in the professional ranks, a new organization man has indeed emerged, one who wants to be an involved father with no loss of income, prestige, and corporate support— and no diminished sense of manhood. Like working women, we want it all. Yet in today's insecure corporate world, we're even less sure of how to get it.

Today's organization man carries a briefcase in one hand and pushes a baby carriage with the other.

Few 1990s men fit the traditional picture of distant father, patriarchal husband, and work-obsessed breadwinner; fewer still have dropped out of the working world completely into full-time daddydom and househusbandhood. Rather than a suburban conformist or high-flying single yuppie, today's organization man carries a briefcase while pushing a baby carriage. He's in his late thirties or forties, balding, perhaps a bit paunchy since there's no time these days for the health club; he no longer wears power ties, and his shirts are rumpled. While he considers his career important, he doesn't want to sacrifice time with his family. His wife may have a demanding job, which he supports; but he may wonder if she thinks he's less of a man than her father, and he may resent her for the time she spends away from home.

Given that most American men grew up believing in the traditional symbols of manhood—wealth, power, status—there are clear emotional and financial costs involved in making other choices. Since many companies still deem dedication to career the sole marker of professional success, the new organization man may believe he has to hide his participation at home. Instead of taking advantage of his company's formal parental-leave policies, for instance, he's more likely to use sick days to watch over a new baby. Even if his boss knows this man is caring for a child and not really sick, the time off is viewed as an exception rather than a threat to the status quo.

With the costs of redefining the male role, however, come the benefits that are driving men to change: as a number of the books reviewed here will show, men who call themselves involved fathers often report that their lives are more meaningful. Some have chosen careers that provide more intrinsic satisfaction, like social work or teaching. Other involved fathers build a sense of who they are outside of work, essentially opting for less demanding jobs or "daddy tracks" that allow for more time with their kids.

But what about those who want both a challenging career and involved fatherhood? Not surprisingly, the compromises made by the new organization man bear a striking resemblance to those of the new organization woman. Because the male experience has been viewed as the norm, many more research studies have been conducted on women's efforts to balance work and family. Yet even if the evidence supporting the changing needs of corporate men is primarily anecdotal, based as it is on interviews and clinical case studies, companies would do well to consider what the new breed of organization man says he wants.

Just as many senior managers now recognize they'll lose their most ambitious women if they don't develop strategies to accommodate family needs, I believe corporations will also lose their best and brightest men if they don't address the needs of the 1990s man.

Who Was the Old Organization Man?

The conventional image of the man in the gray flannel suit emerged in the early 1950s, after the tumult of the Great Depression and World War II. According to the business writer William H. Whyte, Jr., the organization man wanted a settled, stable, suburban existence. Individual expression was cut as short as suburban lawns; these were company men. In Whyte's best-selling and now classic *The Organization Man*, published in 1956, he complained that the rugged individualist had vanished. In his place were workers motivated more by a "passive ambition," those who were "obtrusive in no particular, excessive in no zeal." The future of these organization men would be "a life in which they will all be moved hither and yon and subject to so many forces outside their control."

Whyte's goal in *The Organization Man* was to promote the need for individualism within the context of collective life. For Whyte, increasing collectivization was not a temporary fad but had its roots in the Industrial Revolution and the rise of large corporations and mass production. In addition, the organization man's need to belong derived from one aspect of the U.S. national character: what De Tocqueville called the "special genius" of Americans for cooperative action.

But such belongingness also conflicts with "the public worship of individualism," in Whyte's words, the other side of the American coin. Unquestioning allegiance to the company, then, doesn't jibe with the work ethic of the first U.S. entrepreneurs. And a corporate environment that places emphasis on the primacy of compromise and "group think" certainly doesn't promote the entrepreneurial virtues of hard work and self-reliance.

By the early 1970s, of course, Whyte's organization man no longer matched the economic or social times. Mack Hanan heralded a new arrival in "Make Way for the New Organization Man" (HBR, July–August 1971). Rejecting the comforts of corporate conformity, this new man ran on the fast track. Preoccupied with success, he used the company for his own career advancement as much as the company used him. He was more interested in attaining power than in fitting in.

In this light, the new organization man was back in control of his career, no longer moved "hither and yon" by the inevitable organizational forces described by Whyte. According to Hanan, this new man belonged to himself first and only afterward to his profession, while "corporate belonging often runs . . . a distant fourth, after his sense of social belonging."

During the high-flying 1980s, the image of the career-oriented professional took a back seat to that of the greedy Wall-Streeter popularized by Hollywood. But Hanan's new organization man, having cut his teeth on the political and social movements of the 1960s, was by no means amoral or uncommitted to community. Rather, this man believed in the importance of questioning authority and "that intelligent, consistent dialogue can accelerate institutional change." He fully expected to have more than one career and was most excited by entrepreneurial opportunities within his corporation, such as subsidized start-ups of new businesses. These "corporateurs" didn't necessarily want to start their own companies, but they certainly wanted "to share in the personal benefits of leadership."

Hanan urged companies to take advantage of this new definition of male success by expanding board representation, equity participation, and decentralized decision making; by providing opportunities for collaborative leadership; and by creating an executive fast track that allowed for self-fulfillment through career advancement.

Many U.S. companies have done just that in the name of business necessity and increased productivity. The fast and furious environment of high-tech companies, exemplified by Microsoft, Apple, and Sun Microsystems, has reinforced the image of male business success that is popular today. Whether a programming nerd or a shirt-sleeved manager, he lives and breathes his job because he loves it, even if that means eating takeout in front of his computer every night.

Organization men can no longer count on their careers for self-fulfillment.

But just as the fast-tracker of the 1970s rode roughshod over the conventional organization man Whyte portrayed, today's men are now rebelling against the career expectations that Hanan described. In part, that's because many of the young male professionals of the 1970s and 1980s now have children. While Hanan's men believed in the need for institutional change, his article never questions a system in which only men have careers. Yet today wives work too, and they may be fast-trackers themselves. Most important, given the economic fallout of the 1980s, organization men can no longer count on their careers as an unquestioned source of self-fulfillment—or even as a clear path to financial success.

Manhood Today and the Marketplace

In an expanding economy, hitching one's manhood to a career may make some sense. In a recession, it's a recipe for feelings of failure. A 30-year-old man in 1949 would see his real earnings rise by 63% by the time he turned 40; the same man in 1973 would see his income decline by 1% by his fortieth birthday. Men who are now 30 to 50 years old are the first U.S. generation to be less successful than their fathers were at the same age.[1] As one of the major trends of the past two decades, this economic decline has caused many men to reevaluate work in a harsh new light.

In *The Male Ego*, psychiatrist Willard Gaylin discusses the current erosion of American manhood in three roles: protector, procreator, and, especially, provider. He notes that "nothing is more important to a man's pride, self-respect, status, and manhood than work. Nothing. Sexual impotence, like sudden loss of ambulation or physical strength, may shatter his self-confidence. But . . . pride is built on work and achievement, and the success that accrues from that work. Yet today men often seem confused and contradictory in their attitudes about work."

Gaylin accurately captures the ambivalence and frustration of many men. He says, for example, that "I have never met a man—among my patients or friends—who in his heart of hearts considers himself a success." He satirizes the executive's need for "little pink roses," those pink message slips that tell a man that he's wanted. But when that chairman of the board or CEO finally retires, he suddenly learns he's lost all value. "He becomes a non-person," in Gaylin's words, shocked and overwhelmed by the fact that "he never was someone to be cherished for his own sake but only as an instrument of power and a conduit of goods."

Such strong words sound a bit sweeping; but they do resonate emotionally with the experiences of men who have recently lost their jobs. Indeed, depression is often the result, and as a number of recent studies show, the rate of various forms of depressive illness is on the rise for American men.[2] Gaylin describes self-loathing as one of the hallmarks of depression, a state in which a man tells himself, "I am not dependable; I am a fragile reed. Indeed, I must depend on you." As Gaylin indicates, a man's success is often defined by those around him rather than his own sense of how well he's done. Consider, then, the shaky ground that men are on once they've been laid off. No longer able to provide for their families (or perhaps even themselves), they've lost both their own sense of purpose and their value in society's eyes.

Even men who have achieved success as traditionally defined—such as high-paying executives who can fully provide for their families—may feel that something is missing. Few of the "well-functioning" 80 executives sociologist Robert S. Weiss chose to interview for *Staying the Course*, his insightful if overly celebratory 1990 study, defined themselves by vaulting ambition; most seemed to be content with a kind of grounded stability—being what they called good fathers, good providers, good men. But all of them reported stress and irritability; half had trouble sleeping; most had few close friends, choosing instead to compartmentalize their lives to get through the day.

While they claimed to be devoted fathers and husbands, none of these executives shared housework or child care equally with their wives. Most continued to see their children in economic terms, as "a commitment, an investment, an obligation." Weiss's executives clearly demonstrate how twentieth-century fathers have come to nurture through financial support, a notion that still underpins the prevailing definition of manhood, especially in the corporate arena.

Yet that hasn't always been the case. Historian Robert L. Griswold's impressive 1993 book, *Fatherhood in America*, charts how involved fatherhood has waxed and waned throughout U.S. history. Some middle class eighteenth- and nineteenth-century fathers, for instance, were deeply involved in their children's lives—or at least in the education of their sons. In the early nineteenth century, advice manuals to parents about how to raise their children were addressed primarily to fathers, not mothers.

Although these fathers didn't shoulder domestic responsibilities as their wives did, they were sources of intellectual support. Affectionate bonds were especially strong between fathers and sons; before and during the Civil War, for example, letters from sons were primarily addressed to fathers. But after the war, letters written home were increasingly directed to mothers, as fathers became more remote, enveloped by the rise of the modern corporation and the financial rewards of American Big Business.

Men seek a personal potency that doesn't reside in corporate life itself.

But now the terms have changed again, Griswold argues. The economic need for the two-income couple and women's desires to enter or remain in the labor force

bring men face-to-face with their children in unprecedented ways. And by necessity, men may find a new
sense of purpose through close bonds with their children. One of Griswold's "daddy-trackers," a man who left
a top corporate job to start his own consulting firm comments: "I don't want to make out like I'm a super father
or the perfect husband because that's not true. But I
know I see the kids more now. I coach baseball in the
spring and soccer in the fall because I've got the flexibility in my schedule . . . . I feel a little sorry for men whose
only definition of success is what it says on their business cards."

Given increasing job insecurity, it's no surprise that
men are now searching for ways to control their lives
outside of work. But the daddy-tracker quoted above is
still able to provide for his family. What about men who
have lost their jobs or
don't have the option of
starting their own busi-
ness? What about the
disillusioned yuppies of
the go-go 1980s who are still childless? What about gay
men who are breaking out of stereotypically gay professions? If Hanan's corporateurs searched for a sense of
empowerment on the job, today's men are looking for a
personal potency that doesn't reside in the nature of corporate life itself. But simply switching one's allegiance to
the domestic sphere has its own costs for men. At the
very least, it's easier said than done.

The fact of women in the
workplace has thrown men's
lives into disarray.

Housework: The Final Frontier?

In some respects, William Whyte's organization man *did*
have it all; in the 1950s, it was men who had the careers

and families but only so long as their wives did virtually all of the housework and child care. Whyte's very use of organization man reflects his assumption that the world of work was almost exclusively male, an assumption Hanan carries through in the hard-driving, careerist language of the 1970s. Yet such descriptions, even if they linger in popular culture, hardly match reality today. The entry of women into the workplace is the other major trend pushing men to redefine themselves, whether they want to or not.

Just because so many U.S. women now work doesn't mean that women as a whole care less about nurturing family intimacy. Women not only want both work and family but seem to need both. A number of researchers have discovered that, contrary to conventional wisdom, women who are both employees and mothers often have better self-esteem and experience less stress than those who spend all their time at home with children.[3] But ironically, the very fact of women in the workplace has thrown men's lives into disarray. Now men too face some painful choices. "I want the best of both worlds," says one man to sociologist Kathleen Gerson, author of the significant new book *No Man's Land: Men's Changing Commitments to Family and Work.* "I want to make a lot of money and spend time with my daughter, but obviously I can't have both."

It's not that men don't say they want to change. A 1989 *New York Times* article is typical of the many work-family surveys conducted in recent years: in it, two-fifths of the fathers interviewed said they would quit their jobs if they could spend more time with their children.[4] But the desire to change is often more rhetorical than real; few men would actually switch places with their non-working wives if given the opportunity. In reality, taking on an increasing share of domestic responsibilities usually represents a trade-off. Of the executives Robert Weiss interviewed, those who had won custody of their children took on the parental work of mothers, such as cooking, shopping for clothes, giving baths. Yet Weiss implies that for the few men in his study who were single fathers, their careers suffered. Indeed, in corporations that view family involvement as a blight on performance, a male professional may well believe that investing more energy into the home is a form of treason.

But few men would switch roles with their nonworking spouses . . .

"Housework remains the last frontier that men want to settle," writes Kathleen Gerson. But in this case, "need" may be a better word than "want." No one wants to do housework, but like Mt. Everest, that mountain of unwashed clothing still has to be laundered. Unfortunately, for most male executives, conquering the crabgrass frontier doesn't begin to compare with blazing a trail through the corporate jungle. And there are few social supports available for men's equal participation in domestic life. Male friends don't nod approvingly when men say that they have household chores to finish.

. . . and friends don't nod approvingly when men have housework to do.

In fact, men's share of housework and child care has significantly increased since 1965—from 20% to 30%. But for most men who say they're involved fathers, a sense of domestic purpose begins in the nursery, not in the kitchen or laundry room. Men "make use of various employer policies to accommodate their work role to their family obligations to a far greater degree than is generally realized," reports psychologist Joseph H. Pleck in Jane C. Hood's *Men, Work, and Family,* a useful collection of cutting-edge empirical research on men's shifting priorities on the job and on the domestic front.

As Pleck notes, however, in the absence of corporate or peer-group support, men often do so through less formal channels. For example, a man may take vacation or sick leave to attend to births and the rigors of a young baby. This professional may tell his boss that he's having some tests run and will be in the hospital for a week— wink, wink. Even committed family men may steer clear of parental-leave policies that are essentially intended by top management for women. In addition, while many more men use a company's options for flexible scheduling than paternity leave, they often say it's for another reason besides child care.

Such dissembling is one indication of how little the conception of success on the job has changed—and why men still avoid the domestic responsibilities many say they want. For one thing, housework is not an exciting frontier to conquer but a necessary task to be taken care of. For another, men—and their managers—don't look upon competent homemaking as a badge of masculinity. Last but certainly not least, while current economic and social trends are forcing changes on the home front, the source of meaning in men's lives is open to individual interpretation.

Male Demons and the Search for Meaning

Clearly, the new male ideal is not "Mr. Mom," a simple flip of conventional male and female roles. In fact, rather than accepting the age-old notion that the good man is a family man—and giving it a politically correct 1990s twist—some men may actively rebel against such expectations. The search for meaning outside of family *or* work is by no means new. Despite the ubiquity of the gray flannel suit, 1950s men struggled with the cultural ambivalence created by two male demons: the free loner without obligations and the faceless sheep of the corporation. The demon of defiant nonconformity, personified by Marlon Brando in *The Wild One*, didn't have the self-control necessary to become a responsible adult. Yet the demon of overconformity also haunted male professionals, as organization men of the past worried about losing their individuality and their sense of personal purpose.

> *Men still struggle with the desire to break free, to leave the "rat race," to jump off the fast track.*

Men still struggle with the same desire to break free, to leave the "rat race," to jump off the fast track. *In No Man's Land*, Kathleen Gerson finds that the 138 men she interviewed fall into three categories: breadwinners (36%), autonomous men (30%), and involved fathers (33%). Gerson concludes that, in a recession, becoming an involved father may help redeem a troubled manhood. This new ideal combines both family responsibility and the quest for individuality—the middle ground between undisciplined nonconformity and today's version of the corporate "clone." But it's clear from Gerson's interviews that many men still resist the middle ground.

Gerson's first two groups loosely match the two demons of male identity: overconformers and loners. The first group clings tenaciously to the traditional breadwinner ethic in order to maintain stability and control. Gerson notes that some look back nostalgically "to a time when male advantages were uncontested and supporting a family was an easier task." One of her breadwinners is typical in his assessment of why such an arrangement is fair: "My wife cooks, shops, cleans. I provide the money. To me, to run a home and raise children is a full-time job. If you do more, that's where you lose your children and you lose control."

Gerson's second group of "autonomous" men eschew family obligations altogether, either by remaining single or childless. Wary of intimate attachments, these men consume high-end consumer goods and leisure time. Some have failed in the sexual marketplace, others continue to play the field as contemporary versions of the 1950s playboy. Consider these comments from a 40-year-old computer consultant: "Nobody has a hold on me. I do as I wish, and if tomorrow I don't want to, I don't have to. It's very important that I never feel trapped, locked in."

Many of these men are divorced fathers who no longer contribute to either the financial or emotional support of their children, the "deadbeat dads" of the Clinton era. As Robert Griswold cites in *Fatherhood in America*, nearly two-thirds of all divorced fathers contribute nothing at all to the financial support of their children. Although Gerson calls these men autonomous, they seem more pitiful than free; a deadbeat dad is hardly the archetype of male autonomy.

Some of Gerson's "autonomous" men, being relatively affluent, are indulging in American men's time-honored coping strategy for dealing with conflict in their lives: escape. It's one thing to leave the rat race and find another source of work that's fulfilling; it's quite another to run for the sake of running from family commitments. But in past centuries and decades, American men have left wives and children to go west, to sea, to war, or to any other unblemished arena where a man could find himself and prove his masculine prowess.

At the turn of the century, this search for manhood and autonomy brought American men to fraternal lodges (one in five were members in 1897, according to one observer),[5] while they sent their sons to the Boy Scouts or YMCA as a way to avoid the feminine influence of mothers and wives. Today they're likely to be heading off to the woods with Robert Bly, there to drum, chant, and bond with other men in an evocation of the "deep masculine."

Yet real autonomy isn't the same as escape or disconnection. A truly autonomous man is one who feels in control of what he's doing—be that a high-powered career, a bohemian existence, family life, or some combination of the above. As it turns out, neither Gerson's breadwinners nor "autonomous" men feel especially powerful. One 35-year-old said, "I think it's a tough world to live in. I personally find I'm struggling to do it; why am I going to bring somebody into the world to struggle?" These men feel they've backed into responsibilities reluctantly, either because they became parents against their will or through drifting passively atop an anomic sea of emotional detachment. Neither group believes they actively chose their lives. Theirs is not the life of "quiet desperation" that Thoreau abjured; it's more a life of wistful resignation, of roads not taken.

Not so for the involved fathers, the third group of men Gerson identifies. Most of these men are part of dual-career families. What's more, they have renounced workplace success as the measure of their manhood. One man who had custody of his two children chose to take advantage of his company's early retirement plan because "there's only so far you can go in a corporation, and I reached that level and realized I can't go past it. I realized I paid too high a price for what I got in return. What I got cannot get me back the time with the kids."

Those who do stay in high-pressure workplaces often feel out of step, as this one accountant notes: "I'm a different person at work than I am outside work. When I'm in an environment that somehow nurtures, that somehow is cooperative rather than competitive, it enables me to be a different person, to be myself."

These men most closely fit the image of the new man of the 1990s, both in their embrace of a life outside their jobs and in the difficulties they encounter. Rather than defining themselves rigidly as breadwinners or loners, these men are searching for coherence, for a way to combine the many aspects of their lives. Many of Gerson's involved fathers have

Professionals still confront resistance to change on the job, and much of it comes from top management itself.

left the pitfalls of corporate life altogether, starting their own businesses or going into professions that allow for more flexibility. Through such choices, they avoid putting their manhood on the line when it comes to how their job performance is perceived. But in this respect, the new man isn't an organization man at all. And by placing less emphasis on the importance of work success, these men present a dilemma for corporations that want to retain the best professionals.

The demons of defiance and overconformity continue to haunt men for good reason; in most companies, a man's options seem limited to rebelling or not bucking the system. Before the current economic downturn, the rewards for focusing primarily on career were clear enough, while the benefits of other choices for men often seemed mixed. Although fathers today are most obviously affected by an outmoded image of manhood and professional success, men without children who want other involvements besides a career face similar obstacles. Whether gay or straight, involved fathers or public-service volunteers, male professionals still confront resistance to change on the job, much of it from top management itself.

Resistance to Change: Corporate Inflexibility

The definition of masculinity has proved remarkably inelastic—or, depending on your perspective, amazingly resilient—under its current siege. Except for a few involved fathers, it binds men as tightly as ever to success in the public sphere, in the world of other men, as the markers of manhood and success. "I'm not secure enough, I guess, to stay home and be a househusband," confesses one man, himself an involved father, to Kathleen Gerson.

The traditional definitions of masculinity leave today's new man stranded without social support or a set of viable options. But the real problem, Gerson argues, is institutional. It's corporate inflexibility that reinforces rigid gender definitions. In this, company policies toward family leave exemplify the unconscious assumptions top managers make about what men want—or are supposed to want. A 1989 survey, cited in Joseph Pleck's chapter of *Men, Work, and Family*, found that only 1% of U.S. male employees had access to paid paternity leave, while another 18% had access to unpaid leave. Nine of ten companies made no attempt to inform employees that such leaves were available to new fathers. As a result, we currently have "more reasons to be optimistic about men's desire to nurture children than their opportunity to do so," claims Gerson.

Child care is not simply a women's issue in the workplace anymore; it's a *parents'* issue. Yet the difficulties Gerson's involved fathers face in redefining themselves suggest that companies must do more than provide child care options. Even in Sweden, with its paid parental-leave policies and an official stance on gender equality, men spend more time at work than women do. In another chapter of *Men, Work, and Family*, sociologist Linda Haas reports on whether gender roles in Sweden and other progressive Scandinavian countries differ markedly from those in the United States. To some extent, they do: the participation of Swedish men and women in the labor market is almost identical. But while 43% of Swedish women work part-time, only 7% of the men do. In addition, after government efforts in the late 1980s to increase fathers' participation in family life, the number of Swedish men who took formal parental leave rose to 44%; but again, fathers stayed home with their children for a much shorter time compared with mothers—an average of 43 days rather than 260.

Most telling, some studies have found that Swedish occupations are among the most sex-segregated in the world. Men and women do very different kinds of work at different levels of pay: two-thirds of public-sector employees are women, while only one-third of the private sector are women. Only 3% of Swedish senior executives are women. And in general, an earnings gap of 10% to 30% between men and women exists. As Haas notes of Swedish policymakers,

In fact, the corporate America that was originally designed by men doesn't work anymore for most of us.

"There is no sign that they realize that the benefits to be gained by restructuring work in nongendered ways might outweigh the personal costs to male stakeholders." In other words, business interests still cling to a traditional view of the world, one in which the primacy of men in the corporation remains unchallenged.

In the United States, men now work alongside an increasing number of female colleagues, which has dramatically altered the traditionally all-male arena of the corporation. Such a shift in the workplace has helped to change some old prejudices; but it has also produced a new tension between the sexes, as some men complain that women are competing for "their" jobs. Gerson's breadwinners, for example, resent women's entry into the workplace, holding fast to the solace of the all-male public arena before it was "invaded" by women. In this context, sexual harassment will continue to be a significant problem for working women. Such harassment is a way for men to remind women that they are, after all, "just" women who happen to be in the workplace but don't really belong there.

The cause of such bitterness and uncertainty, however, lies not in the supposed new power of women but in the rapid changes taking place in today's corporations. In fact, the Corporate America originally designed by men doesn't work anymore for most of us. The tension and low morale now found in many large companies reflect the clash between the need for organizational change and the old ideology. On the one hand, companies furiously restructure and reengineer work to match a new information economy and more diverse labor force; on the other hand, the perceived costs of being an involved father—loss of income, male comradeship, and manhood—remain real because the traditional view of what makes a professional successful hasn't changed.

Make Way for the New Employee

For obvious reasons, men who believe their lives are meaningful are likely to have the strongest sense of self-esteem. Compared with Gerson's so-called "autonomous" men, many of whom expressed frustration about their claustrophobic jobs and irritating coworkers, the involved men had a much clearer sense of why they had made the choices they did. And according to Gerson and other researchers, these men say they're more productive workers, better managers, and more creative team players. Gerson reports that the involved fathers she interviewed tended to be the most egalitarian, especially when it came to the right of women to pursue their own careers. Thus these men are the most respectful of female colleagues in the workplace. Since involved fathers and husbands appear to be the most emotionally flexible employees, they're in the best position to make the kinds of changes corporations now require.

Given the prevailing atmosphere of job insecurity, companies need to become increasingly creative in developing ways for their employees to feel good about themselves and their work. As Joseph Pleck notes, Malcolm Forbes's 1986 declaration— "new daddies need paternity leave like they need a hole in the head"—seems as false for today's employers as it is for today's employees. Still,

Yet companies can encourage a new kind of male-female comradeship at work.

it's not enough for senior managers to put enlightened parental-leave and flexible-scheduling policies on the books. If Gerson's involved fathers are to stay in the organization, they must feel comfortable using those policies. And they must believe their job performance is evaluated fairly, not based on old conceptions of the male breadwinner.

Perhaps a professional's willingness to move to another city, for instance, isn't the best demonstration of his or her motivation. Basing promotions on how many weeks an employee spends working 16-hour days may lead to burnout rather than increased productivity, let alone creativity. In addition, not every male professional wants to be on a management track, though most still believe the work they do defines an important part of who they are. Certainly, some men and some women may always be more career-oriented than others are. Indeed, companies may require a certain number of fast-trackers to get the job done. But whether those people should be men or women is still based more on out-moded gender stereotypes than economic sense.

At the very least, companies can encourage a new kind of male-female comradeship at work, as does Silicon Valley's Organizational Development Network. As the current flood of diversity training attests, there are undoubtedly new difficulties in the workplace as male employees wrestle with both job insecurity and the increasing presence of female colleagues. But even if top managers bring in diversity trainers to help people work together, many still fail to examine their own attitudes about what it means to be a success. And it's in changing the larger framework for viewing employee loyalty and commitment that managers will bring about the biggest changes.

When Mack Hanan announced the arrival of the new organization man in 1971, he was right to call forth a new vision of the empowered corporateur: a professional who wanted to control his own career, who would be motivated by equity participation and the opportunity to take creative leaps, not just the stability of a monthly paycheck. Today's professionals still want much of what Hanan suggested corporations give them. Many certainly want the chance to run on a fast track, at least at some point in their working lives. By necessity, most of them are learning to live with economic insecurity, as long as companies reward their performance adequately.

Yet in Hanan's hierarchy of belonging, family didn't figure at all; in fact, he never even mentions the word in his article. In the 1990s, companies can no longer take for granted that family life is the exclusive domain of women. For the new man—that is, the new employee—family and career often receive equal weight. Freud himself suggested a similar prescription for the healthy person: "Lieben und arbeiten." Love and work.

But Hanan's sense of "social belonging" also has its place in the new mix. Rather than simply retreating into family life as a way to avoid the disappointments of the current workplace, today's men can find meaning through involvement with the larger world as well. A balance of career, family, and community suggests more than a hierarchy in which one occupation takes precedence over everything else; a life focused on more than just work—or family—can provide a stable foundation for every man's personal definition of success.

Suggested Readings

The Organization Man
by William H. Whyte, Jr.
New York: Simon and Schuster, 1956.

"Make Way for the New Organization Man"
by Mack Hanan
Harvard Business Review
July–August 1971.

The Male Ego
by Willard Gaylin
New York: Viking, 1992.

Staying the Course: The Emotional and Social Lives of Men Who Do Well at Work
by Robert S. Weiss
New York: The Free Press, 1990.

Fatherhood in America: A History
by Robert L. Griswold
New York: BasicBooks, 1993.

No Man's Land: Men's Changing Commitments to Family and Work
by Kathleen Gerson
New York: BasicBooks, 1993.

Men, Work, and Family
edited by Jane C. Hood
Newbury Park: Sage Publications, 1993.

"Are 'Family-Supportive' Employer Policies Relevant to Men?"
by Joseph H. Pleck
in Hood (above).

"Nurturing Fathers and Working Mothers: Changing Gender Roles in Sweden"
by Linda Haas
in Hood (previous page).

Notes

1. See Katherine Newman, *Falling from Grace* (New York: Free Press, 1990) and *Declining Fortunes: The Withering of the American Dream* (BasicBooks, 1993) for an extended discussion of the declining fortunes of the American middle class.

2. Cross-National Collaborative Group, "The Changing Rate of Major Depression: Cross-National Comparisons," *Journal of the American Medical Association*, December 2, 1992, pp. 3098-3105; Gerald L. Klerman and Myrna M. Weissman, "Increasing Rates of Depression," JAMA, April 21, 1989, pp. 2229-2235; and Priya J. Wickramaratne, Myrna M. Weissman, Philip J. Leap, and Theodore R. Holford, "Age, Period, and Cohort Effects on the Risk of Major Depression: Results from Five United States Communities," *Journal of Clinical Epidemiology*, Vol. 42, No. 4, 1989, pp. 333-343.

3. See Faye J. Crosby's *Juggling: The Unexpected Advantages of Balancing Career and Home for Women and Their Families* (New York: Free Press, 1991) for an overview of the research done on women, work, and family. Among the many pioneering researchers Crosby cites are Rosalind Barnett and Grace Baruch.

4. Lisa Belkin, "Bars to Equality of Sexes Seen as Eroding, Slowly," *New York Times*, August 20, 1989, p. A1, A26.

5. W. Harwood, "Secret Societies in America," *North American Review*, 1897. This article and others are also discussed in Mark Carnes's *Fraternal Ritual and Manhood in Victorian America*, Yale University Press, 1989.

Originally published in November–December 1993
Reprint 93606

The Alternative Workplace

Changing Where and How People Work

MAHLON APGAR IV

Executive Summary

TODAY MANY ORGANIZATIONS, including AT&T and IBM, are pioneering the *alternative workplace*—the combination of nontraditional work practices, settings, and locations that is beginning to supplement traditional offices. This is not a fad. Although estimates vary widely, it is safe to say that some 30 million to 40 million people in the United States are now either telecommuters or home-based workers.

What motivates managers to examine how people spend their time at the office and where else they might do their work? Among the potential benefits for companies are reduced costs, increased productivity, and an edge in vying for and keeping talented employees. They can also capture government incentives and avoid costly sanctions. But at the same time, alternative workplace programs are not for everyone. Indeed, such

155

programs can be difficult to adopt, even for those organizations that seem to be most suited to them. Ingrained
behaviors and practical hurdles are hard to overcome.
And the challenges of managing both the cultural
changes and systems improvements required by an alternative workplace initiative are substantial.

How should senior managers think about alternative
workplace programs? What are the criteria for determining whether the alternative workplace is right for a
given organization? What are the most common pitfalls
in implementing alternative workplace programs? The
author provides the answers to these questions in his
examination of this new frontier of where and how people work.

On SEPTEMBER 20, 1994, some 32,000 AT&T
employees stayed home. They weren't sick or on strike.
They were telecommuting. Employees ranging from the
CEO to phone operators were part of an experiment that
involved 100,000 people. It's purpose? To explore how
far a vast organization could go in transforming the
workplace by moving the work to the worker instead of
the worker to work.

Today AT&T is just one among many organizations
pioneering the *alternative workplace* (AW)—the combination of nontraditional work practices, settings, and
locations that is beginning to supplement traditional
offices. This is not a fad. Although estimates vary widely,
some 30 million to 40 million people in the United States
are now either telecommuters or home-based workers.

What motivates managers to examine how people
spend their time at the office and where else they could

work? The most obvious reason is cost reduction. Since 1991, AT&T has freed up some $550 million in cash flow—a 30% improvement—by eliminating offices people don't need, consolidating others, and reducing related overhead costs. Through an AW program called the Mobility Initiative, IBM is saving more than $100 million annually in its North America sales and distribution unit alone.

Another reason is the potential to increase productivity. Employees in the alternative workplace tend to devote less time and energy to typical office routines and more to customers. At IBM, a survey of employees in the Mobility Initiative revealed that 87% believe that their personal productivity and effectiveness on the job have increased significantly.

The alternative workplace also can give companies an edge in vying for—and keeping—talented, highly motivated employees. American Express president and COO Kenneth I. Chenault says that AmEx's AW initiatives help the company retain experienced employees who find the flexibility to work from home especially attractive.

Finally, AW programs are beginning to offer opportunities to capture government incentives and avoid costly sanctions. Many communities are easing zoning rules to enable more residents to establish home offices. In addition, companies are meeting Clean Air Act requirements—and avoiding hefty fines—through regional workplace strategies with extensive AW components. Finally, tax codes may change to enable more employees to deduct home office costs.

The potential benefits are clear. But at the same time, AW programs are not for everyone. Indeed, such programs can be difficult to adopt, even for those organizations most suited to them. Ingrained behaviors and practical hurdles are hard to overcome. And the challenges of managing both the cultural changes and the systems improvements required by an AW initiative are substantial.

How should senior managers think about AW programs? What are the criteria for determining whether the alternative workplace is right for a given organization? What are the most common pitfalls in implementation? The lessons learned by managers who have successfully launched such programs and by those who are struggling to do so suggest that the best place to start is with a clear understanding of the many forms an alternative workplace can take. (See "Myths About the Alternative Workplace" at the end of this article.)

A Spectrum of Options

Different companies use different variations on the AW theme to tailor new work arrangements to their own needs. To one company, for example, establishing an alternative workplace may mean simply having some workers on different shifts or travel schedules share desks and office space. AT&T determined that for some groups of employees, up to six people could use the same desk and equipment formerly assigned to one. The company now has 14,000 employees in shared-desk arrangements.

Replacing traditional private offices with open-plan space is another option. In such arrangements, a company typically provides team rooms and workstations in open areas. Free-address facilities are a variation on that format. As Jill M. James, director of AT&T's Creative Workplace Solutions initiative, describes them, "You are assigned to one facility, but you can move around and choose a variety of work settings during the day. You don't have to log in or put your name tag on a specific work space. And everyone can find you because your phone, pager, and PC go with you."

Some companies have embraced the concept of "hoteling." As in the other shared-office options, "hotel" work spaces are furnished, equipped, and supported with typical office services. Employees may have mobile cubbies, file cabinets, or lockers for personal storage; and a computer system routes phone calls and E-mail as necessary. But "hotel" work spaces are reserved by the hour, by the day, or by the week instead of being permanently assigned. In addition, a "concierge" may provide employees with travel and logistical support. At its most advanced, "hotel" work space is customized with individuals' personal photos and memorabilia, which are stored electronically, retrieved, and "placed" on occupants' desktops just before they arrive, and then removed as soon as they leave.

Satellite offices are another form of alternative workplace. Such offices break up large, centralized facilities into a network of smaller workplaces that can be located close to customers or to employees' homes. Satellites can save a company up to 50% in real estate costs, diversify the risk of overconcentration in a single location, and broaden the pool of potential employees. Some are shells—sparsely furnished and equipped with only basic technology; others are fully equipped and serviced. Satellites are generally located in comparatively inexpensive cities and suburban areas. Most often, they have simpler and less costly furnishings and fixtures than their downtown counterparts.

The U.S. Army's General Reimer rapidly receives on-line advice from officers around the globe.

Telecommuting is one of the most commonly recognized forms of alternative workplace. Telecommuting—that is, performing work electronically wherever the worker chooses—generally supplements the traditional workplace rather than replacing it. At IBM, however, telecommuters comprise an entire business unit. And at PeopleSoft, telecommuting is the dominant style of work throughout the entire company.

General Dennis J. Reimer, the U.S. Army's chief of staff, offers compelling insight into what an executive can do from a remote location. Reimer travels with a laptop and routinely communicates by E-mail with 350 general officers and 150 garrison commanders around the world. Using a Web-based network called America's Army On-line, which also includes an intranet chat room similar to those offered through commercial providers, Reimer can raise issues with his officers and receive advice on key decisions, often within hours. "The network allows me to be productive and to maintain a pulse on what is happening whether I'm in Washington or overseas," Reimer says. "It not only saves travel costs but also enables collaborative teamwork across organizational and geographic boundaries around the globe. Gradually, this is changing the culture from one in which 'my information is power' to one in which 'sharing is power.'"

Home offices complete the spectrum of AW options. Companies vary widely in their approaches to home offices. Some simply allow certain employees to work at home at their own discretion and at their own expense. Others—such as AT&T, IBM, and Lucent Technologies—provide laptops, dedicated phone lines, software support, fax-printer units, help lines, and full technical backup at the nearest corporate facility. One major company goes still further by providing employees who work at home with a $1,000 allowance for furnishings and equipment to be used at their discretion. Most organizations find that a mix of AW options is better than a one-size-fits-all approach. Indeed, the very concept of the alternative workplace means tailoring the program to an organization's specific needs. AT&T's Creative Workplace Solutions strategy, for example, combines three options: shared offices, telecommuting, and virtual offices. These options can accommodate nearly all of AT&T's office-based functions. (See "AT&T's First Shared Office" at the end of this article.)

Is the Alternative Workplace Right for Your Organization?

The first step toward determining whether any or all of the AW options I've outlined could work for your organization is to answer a few basic questions.

Are you committed to new ways of operating? For example, are you prepared to overhaul performance measures as necessary to align them with the new ways in which employees work? Are you braced for a cultural tailspin as your employees learn new ways of connecting with one another from afar? Are you committed to examining your incentives and rewards policies in light of the different ways in which work may be completed? Consider what Kevin Rirey, an IBM marketing manager, said about performance measurement and rewards in his unit after the Mobility Initiative was put in place: "We've always rewarded for results, but when you are in a traditional office environment and see the effort that people put into a job, it's very difficult not to reward them at least partly for that effort. We don't tend to do that anymore. We focus a lot more on results than on effort. But it's a difficult transition."

Is your organization *informational* rather than *industrial*? This distinction refers to a management philosophy and style rather than to an economic sector or customer base. *Industrial* in this context means that the organization's structure, systems, and management processes are designed for intensive face-to-face interaction and that employees remain rooted to specific workplaces. In such an environment, the potential for AW arrangements is limited.

Informational organizations, by contrast, operate mainly through voice and data communications when it comes to both their employees and their customers. *Informational*, as used here, does not necessarily mean high-tech. But it does mean that managers and employees are moving up the curve toward information-age literacy, which is characterized by flexibility, informality, the ability to change when necessary, respect for personal time and priorities, and a commitment to using technology for improving performance.

Until recently, AT&T and IBM were among the many companies perceived by customers and analysts as industrial organizations; that is, they were seen as tradition bound, formal, bureaucratic, and slow to change. As former AT&T chairman Robert Allen noted on the company's Telecommuting Day in 1994, "Work is where the phone is, and it's logical that we should work like a phone-based organization. When our initiative began, however, AT&T looked like an antiquated company, with fixed schedules, expensive space, and a heavy hierarchy." When the two companies launched their AW programs nearly ten years ago, top-level managers had already begun to reposition their organizations as informational.

Do you have an open culture and proactive managers? A dynamic, nonhierarchical, technologically advanced organization is more likely than a highly structured, command-driven one to implement an AW program successfully. That's why so many newer and smaller companies—particularly those that are heavily involved in the business of information or in electronic commerce—are using AW techniques with great success and with few transition pains. Yet as we've seen, even tradition-conscious organizations can use such techniques to eliminate fixed costs and facilitate performance improvements. The key is whether managers at all levels are open to change.

Richard Karl Goeltz, vice chairman and CFO of American Express, comments, "It's important to have a multifunction team of senior managers promoting and supporting a virtual-office initiative right from the start. We had three departments involved in our effort: HR, technology, and real estate. The individuals on the team must be enthusiastic and not unnecessarily fettered by traditional approaches. And they must be made knowledgeable about all the key issues—from the ways in which corporate policies may be redefined to deal with various types of problems and opportunities to the different options for providing furniture or allowances to employees. Still, I would be skeptical about whether management by fiat would work very well. It's better to be able to say, 'Here's an opportunity to enable you to do your job better, more efficiently, and more economically. You don't have to use it, but it's here.' What I've seen happen elsewhere—and we're beginning to see it in our own initiatives—is that once a fairly large department takes the first step, others are quick to follow."

Can you establish clear links between staff, functions, and time? AW programs assume that certain jobs either do not depend on specific locations and types of facilities or depend on them only part of the time. To analyze whether an AW program can work in your company, you must understand in detail the parameters of each job you are considering for the program. What function does the job serve? Is the work performed over the phone? In person? Via computer? All of the above? How much time does the employee need to spend in direct contact with other employees, customers, and business contacts? Is the location of the office critical to performance? Does it matter whether the job is 9 to 5? Is it important for others to be able to reach the employee immediately?

Managers who assume that the alternative workplace suits only road warriors on the sales force may be in for a surprise.

If a critical mass of corporate functions cannot work in an AW environment, the potential benefits may be too marginal relative to the required investment and effort. But managers who assume intuitively that an AW initiative is limited only to road warriors on the sales force may be surprised; often, more jobs are suited to a different way of working than at first seems possible. Executives at Dun and Bradstreet, for example, initially thought that only 5% of their global workforce could be involved in an AW program but learned that two-fifths of the company's functions—involving half their employees—could adapt with only minor adjustments in work practices.

Are you prepared for some "push back"? As Lorraine Fenton, vice president of information technology for IBM North America observes, most "twenty-some-things" entering the workforce have never had a private office, so to begin their work life without one is not a traumatic change. But for many employees, the transition from conventional to alternative workplaces is not as easy. Employees who are accustomed to a structured office environment may find it hard to adjust to a largely self-directed schedule, and those who are used to working within earshot of many colleagues may be lonely in a remote setting. Moreover, middle managers, who lose their visual and verbal proximity to their direct reports, have to change the way in which they relate to those employees. In fact, middle managers usually put up the strongest resistance to the alternative workplace, in large part because they feel as though the very foundations of their roles are being pulled out from under them.

Can you overcome the external barriers to an AW program? Even if the work is suited to an AW format and managers and employees alike are amenable to change, physical and logistical barriers may exist. If space is at a premium in employees' homes—for example, if many employees live in small apartments—then an AW initiative that calls for people to work at home may not be feasible. This is a key consideration in U.S. cities and in most countries abroad. In Japan, for instance, there simply is no "swing" space in most employees' homes that could be used as office space; to accommodate a home-office initiative there, employees would have to sacrifice living space. Conducting employee focus groups at the exploratory and planning stages of an AW initiative can uncover such concerns effectively.

Will you invest in the tools, training, and techniques that make AW initiatives work? To improve the chances of an AW program's success, all who are involved must be armed with a full set of tools; relevant training; and appropriate, flexible administrative support. Are you committed, for example, to providing standardized computer software for people working in all locations? Accessible, qualified technical assistance? Do you have the financial resources to provide the above?

Too many AW programs are undertaken with only partial support from the organization. Confusion and frustration inevitably ensue, not to mention drops in productivity. These programs are only marginally successful and might ultimately fail. When an employee at home can't communicate with other employees or clients, access the right information, or easily reach a help desk to solve a technology problem, the initiative is destined to fail. As AT&T's James puts it, "The technology has to work from the start. When you're asking people to give up their space and all that goes with it, you owe it to them to make sure that the systems are flawless. Because employees are mobile, the tools they use are their lifeline. They can't survive without them."

If you have answered "yes" to the foregoing questions, you could seriously consider an AW program. The next step is to drill down into the economics of AW initiatives.

Tangible and Intangible Economics

As I suggested earlier, the main reason for AW programs is to reduce current costs and avoid future ones. For established organizations that are pressed for cash, the savings from relinquishing space and making better use of what remains can dwarf the necessary investment in equipment and training. For young organizations, an AW program can give managers a viable alternative to expensive, long-term lease commitments.

But for the typical enterprise, the economics of the alternative workplace are more complex, and the decision to adopt an AW program rests as much—or more—on intangibles as it does on simple financials. Jerome T. Roath, IBM's manager of infrastructure expense, says, "The obvious savings from real-estate cost reduction may hide qualitative improvements in employee satisfaction and customer service that are less measurable but no less important and in the end might justify an [AW] program."

On the flip side, AmEx's Goeltz comments on how a business might think about satellite locations: "Instead of 2,000 people concentrated in one place, one could consider 100 sites of 20 people each around the country. That might cut real estate costs tremendously. But there would be other critical issues to address. For example, would the company provide cafeteria and health club facilities or instead provide allowances to help people pay for their own? And how does one coordinate HR activities across a dispersed group?"

Managers should look at the economics of a potential AW program from three perspectives—the company's, the employee's, and the customer's—and weigh the tangible and intangible costs against the respective benefits. Tangible setup costs for the company include hardware, software, training, and any equipment or furniture the company provides; ongoing costs include allowances, phone charges, and technical support. In home offices, employees provide their own space and some, if not all, of the furnishings and equipment. Intangible costs for the company and its employees include the time spent learning new work habits and ways of communicating with colleagues and customers.

The act of removing the walls that separate people in traditional offices can foster teamwork.

Aside from real estate savings, the organization benefits from increased employee productivity, recruiting, and retention—usually because AW employees have both more professional and more personal time. In one AT&T unit, for example, the average AW participant gained almost five weeks per year by eliminating a 50-minute daily commute. Employees in home offices and other remote locations also can be more efficient during the workday because they have fewer distractions and less downtime. As AT&T's James notes, "When I have 30 minutes between meetings, I can load in my disk and be productive on the spot." Customer satisfaction also improves: as customers become comfortable communicating with the organization electronically, they can reach employees more quickly and receive more direct, personal attention.

Intangible benefits include closer teamwork and greater flexibility. The simple act of removing the walls that separate people in traditional private offices often fosters teamwork. Stephen M. Brazzell, AT&T's vice president for global real estate, says, "Connectivity between individuals and groups comes in many forms, both physical and electronic. Those in shared offices tell us, 'The new arrangement works. It really helps us communicate quickly and effectively because we're all together.' There is a definite improvement in communication, and communication means productivity." What's more, meetings in the alternative workplace take less time because participants manage their time better; they meet not just to discuss issues but to resolve them.

The U.S. Army's Reimer highlights the importance of intangible benefits in his widely dispersed organization: "The biggest benefit I have found is that leaders who are 'far from the flagpole' in places like Bosnia and Korea have direct access to me and to my latest thoughts on many issues. In turn, I receive feedback from the field army as quickly as I would from my staff at the Pentagon. This empowers our leadership team, and it allows the army to speak and act with one voice on rapidly changing situations."

A crucial intangible benefit of an AW program is the value that employees place on increased personal time and control. Although they tend to work longer hours and may even have difficulty leaving their home offices, AW employees find the promise of flexibility attractive, so they are easier to recruit and retain. As Reimer says, "We are now training soldiers when and where it is needed. This not only reduces costs and improves readiness, but it also reduces the time soldiers spend away from home and family—an ever-increasing burden with our intensive training and operational requirements. This helps us retain quality soldiers and their families."

The chart "AT&T's Creative Workplace Plan" illus-
trates one company's assessment of its tangible economics. Over the next five years, AT&T's initiative is
expected to generate annual savings of nearly $50
million as people become accustomed to and take full
advantage of the new style of working. This will be a
substantial contribution to AT&T's overall aim of reducing annual occupancy costs by $200 million. The plan
begins by defining the ratio of occupants to work space
for each type of office, the square feet and cost per person, and the expected savings and payback. Shared-
office and virtual-office workers use one-third to one-
tenth as much corporate space as they do in traditional
offices. Over time, these changes could yield annual savings of $5,000 to $10,000 per person. For a group of 100
employees occupying space that costs $24 per square
foot, the savings range from $200,000 to $600,000, and
payback ranges from one to three years. AT&T's James,
who authored the plan, estimates that some 34,000
employees—one-fourth of the total—could be accom-
modated in AW settings by 2003.

IBM's experience in the alternative workplace provides another good example of well-balanced cost-benefit
ratios. IBM began piloting various AW options in 1989 to
reduce real-estate–related costs and to explore the use of
technology to support sales. But by 1993, the company's
profitability and competitiveness had declined to the
point that more fundamental changes in corporate strategy were called for. In that context, the early pilot projects were transformed into a mainstream initiative in
the North America sales and service organization—an
initiative designed to improve customer responsiveness,
reduce costs, and increase productivity.

AT&T's Creative Workplace Plan

AT&T's five-year plan reflects the significant impact of creative workplace initiatives on reducing total occupancy costs. The financial benefits result from five interrelated factors to be implemented over time: shifting from traditional to shared and virtual offices, adopting more efficient individual workspace designs, improving office utilization, reducing total company space, and adjusting the number of occupants using company space. The plan's current benchmarks and overall projections are summarized below.

Benchmarks

Office Type	Utilization ratio	Square feet per person	$ per person (setup)	$ per person[1] (annual)	$ per unit[2] (annual)	Payback (years)
			Cost		**Savings**	
Traditional	1:1	225	12,000	12,000	NA	NA
Shared	3:1	125	7,500	9,000	450,000	1.4
Virtual	10:1	30	5,000	6,000	600,000	0.8

Projections

Factor	Traditional	Shared	Virtual	Total	Traditional	Shared	Virtual	Total	Total	CWP
	1998				**2002**				**Differences[3]**	
Square feet (millions)	28.5	2.8	0.6	31.9	18.3	2.0	0.6	20.9	-11.0	-2.9
Square feet per person	300	200	150	285 (average)	225	125	30	190 (average)	-95	-96
Number of occupants	95,000	14,000	4,000	113,000	81,000	20,000	10,000	111,000	-2,000	+12,000
Annual savings ($ millions)	NA	NA	NA	NA	153	30	19	202	-202	-49

Notes:
1. This metric includes real estate as well as voice and data communications costs.
2. This metric is based on a 100-person unit occupying leased space at $24 per square foot.
3. Differences for each factor reflect the changes in the total portfolio from January 1, 1998 to December 31, 2002. They also reflect the changes attributable to the creative workplace initiative during the same period.

Lee A. Dayton, IBM's vice president for corporate development and real estate, recalls, "Two principles were—and are—at the heart of the initiative. First, we want to reduce our employees' travel time. When they are traveling from one customer to another, or from the IBM office to the customer, they're not productive. Second, if employees are at home or at a customer's office, we want to eliminate the need to travel to an IBM office. And if they're not going to work in an IBM office, we want to eliminate the dedicated space with all of its overhead and services."

Currently, IBM's entire U.S. sales force can operate independent of a traditional workplace. More than 12,500 employees have given up their dedicated work spaces, and another 13,000 are capable of mobile operation. IBM also has implemented mobility initiatives, involving some 15,000 employees in Asia, Europe, and Latin America. Thus, approximately 17% of IBM's total worldwide workforce is sufficiently equipped and trained to work in AW formats, and one-third of all the company's departments have at least some mobile employees.

The results? In 1992, worldwide occupancy and voice-IT expenses (that is, phone-based communication charges) totaled $5.7 billion. By 1997, the total had dropped 42% to $3.3 billion. During that period, real estate savings totaled $1 billion from mobility initiatives alone. Even more telling, worldwide costs per person declined 38% from $15,900 to $9,800, and the combined ratio of occupancy and voice-IT expenses to revenues dropped from 8.8% to 4.2%—a 52% improvement. (See the chart "The Economics of Mobility at IBM North America" for a breakdown of these measures.)

As Roath comments, IBM must keep close watch over voice-IT charges. They are still small compared with occupancy costs and other IT expenses, but they could explode as more people go mobile. Still, Dayton says, "The costs you incur with mobility—IT technology, communications, wireless costs—are all going down, while the relative costs of real estate continue to rise." Dayton also notes that the key to success is evaluating and managing the initiative with the ultimate business goal in mind: "We cost-justified our program based on reductions in spending, primarily from real estate. From the start, we allowed business managers to make the trade-off between real estate savings and investments in technology. And we insisted on saving more than we spent. Every laptop and cellular phone we bought for the initiative was cost-justified. We also introduced an annual worldwide scorecard that tallied cost and square feet per person. The scorecard applied to manufacturing and development departments as well as to sales and distribution. We published the results internally, and, of course, nobody wanted to be last."

Looking ahead, John Newton, IBM's manager of IT plans and measurements, believes that the company's extraordinary cost savings will plateau: "The main short-term problem in mobility economics is that as more people go mobile, we still need a support structure for them. We are reaching a point of diminishing returns, because we can't keep pulling people out of offices forever. There will be productivity benefits but not occupancy cost savings."

Indeed, any organization adopting an AW initiative can be expected to reach a new plateau—with lower fixed costs, higher productivity, and greater employee and customer satisfaction than it previously experienced. But by redeploying some of the savings into better equipment, technical support, even the company picnic, the organization that benefits from AW initiatives can realize further dividends in employee commitment and loyalty.

Implementing an AW Initiative

If the economics are favorable, you should consider implementing an AW initiative. The following guidelines will help you chart your course.

The Economics of Mobility at IBM North America

Total Occupancy and Voice-IT Costs

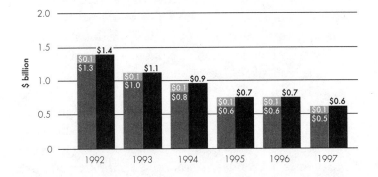

Occupancy and Voice-IT Costs per Person

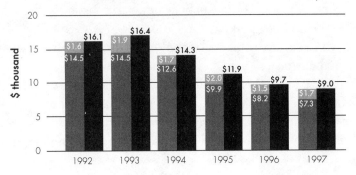

**Start with a pilot project and don't overcompli-
cate it.** An AW program can be designed either for
pilot testing or for full implementation. The choice
will depend on many factors. If a company is hemor-
rhaging, then a full-scale rollout makes sense: the need
for radical change to reduce costs will be clearly and
universally understood. And if the company already is
informational, with a large number of travelers and
independent workers, then the risk of failing at full

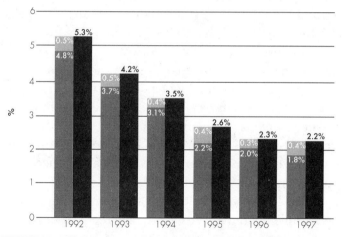

Occupancy and Voice-IT Costs as a Percentage of Revenue

Voice-IT Costs

Occupancy Costs

Total Costs

*IBM's entire U.S. sales force can operate independent of a
traditional office. More than 12,500 employees have given up
their dedicated work spaces, and another 13,000 are capable
of mobile operation. Managers monitor the performance of the
company's Mobility Initiative in several ways, including those
illustrated at left and above.*
*The top left chart shows the total occupancy and voice-IT costs for IBM North America.
The bottom left chart, which breaks down those costs by employee, helps managers
assess whether the Mobility Initiative is using space, information, and communications
efficiently. The chart above, which shows total occupancy and voice-IT costs as a percentage of IBM North America's revenue, helps managers assess the productivity and
efficiency of the Mobility Initiative.*

implementation is low. For most organizations, however, an AW program involves so many innovations
and departures from

A phased approach to an AW program is essential in order to test what's acceptable.

deeply held norms that a phased, experimental approach is essential to test what's acceptable and to change what isn't. Because this is not "business as usual," it will take extra management time and attention, talented staff, experienced consultants, and some expense to ensure success.

It's a good idea to begin with obvious functions—such as personal sales, telemarketing, project engineering, and consulting—in which individuals already work with their clients by phone or at the clients' premises. Such employees are largely self-directed and need only their phones and laptops to operate in the alternative workplace. Their input could be decisive in ensuring a successful project. In fact, IBM's Dayton credits much of the success of his company's initiative to the fact that it was a bottom-up effort. "We provided direction from the top about our goals," he explains, "but we went deep into the organization to make the program work. Relatively low-level people helped plan it, and local management implemented it. We encouraged them to experiment. It was a peer-driven effort by and for the people who were going to be affected."

David House, president of Establishment Services Worldwide at American Express, began an alternative workplace initiative in 1993 with a pilot project for 300 sales and account service reps in 85 field offices throughout the United States. (See "How Senior Executives at American Express View the Alternative Workplace" at the end of this article.) By 1995, only 7 offices were needed, the participants were enthusiastic, and customer satisfaction rates had improved. Based on that sucess, a second pilot project was launched at the New York headquarters—a much tougher challenge. Alan Haber, AmEx's project director, says, "The savings from a virtual-office program are much greater at headquarters than in the field offices because we have so much infrastructure and administrative support here. But there's also more resistance to virtual offices. Many people like to come to this building and don't want to give it up."

In foreign operations, pilot projects can be particularly valuable because they allow a company the freedom to experiment in an environment in which cultural and physical differences can be profound. For example, a proactive approach that works in the United States may be counterproductive or downright destructive abroad. The AW concept can best be nurtured in small-scale situations where the local leadership is enthusiastic, the employees are willing to innovate, and the work environment is conducive to change.

Segment the workforce you are considering for the alternative workplace, and assess the logistics of the proposed new arrangement. Whether you're designing a pilot project or rolling out a full program, the first step is to divide the target employees into three segments that define their ties to the workplace: office bound, travel driven, and independent. Employees are best grouped by position rather than by individual, and jobs should be analyzed in as much detail as the data allow. Figuring out the logistics of how employees will work together when they are no longer rooted to a traditional setting is a more straightforward task if you have a clear idea of what they currently do and how and when they do it. Various AW formats can apply to each segment, so the sharper this analysis, the easier it will be to design an appropriate program. The criteria below are not hard-and-fast definitions but guidelines that each organization should adapt to its own situation.

Office-bound staff members spend nearly all their time in a single, fixed, assigned location, whether they are working alone or as part of a team. Their workplace is typically composed of private offices, workstations or "cubes," and meeting rooms. The more these spaces are clustered, the more team interaction occurs, but the harder it is to ensure individuals' privacy. For office-bound workers, desk sharing may be applied in multi-shift operations where work patterns are predictable. For example, two or three people could be assigned to the same office or workstation during daily shifts in a round-the-clock operation, or up to six people could use the same space on different days of the week.

Travel-driven staff members spend at least half their time visiting sites outside their assigned locations, usually for transactions and projects. In fact, their performance is based largely on their capacity to spend as much time outside the office as possible, either with clients (for those in sales and consulting) or while working on projects (for auditors and engineers). Technology can release these travelers almost entirely from their assigned workplaces because they need face-to-face time with clients and colleagues.

Independent employees can set up anywhere and anytime with a computer, modem, and telephone line. In contrast to the other two segments, these employees do not need to be physically present at specific locations. They do not depend on direct contact with clients or colleagues, so they do not need dedicated, preassigned work spaces. Writers, consultants, and scholars are traditional examples of the independent worker. Today,

Monitoring the performance of people you can't see is not easy. Set clear goals from the outset, or your employees may founder.

however, individuals in many functions can work independently even though they are members of large, interdependent enterprises. Such people often favor a home office to avoid interruptions; to be close to their families; and to eliminate the time, expense, and stress of commuting. Independent workers also enjoy the freedom to set up their work space according to their personal tastes—an opportunity not offered in most corporate environments where uniform layouts and standard furnishings are the norm.

Make sure that managers and employees are clear both on performance objectives and on how performance will be measured. In a traditional office, checking on employees' day-to-day progress and altering the course of their work is a relatively straightforward process. But monitoring the performance of people you can't see is quite different. It is all too easy for an employee to founder for some time without his or her manager's knowledge. Setting clear goals from the outset— and agreeing on a way to monitor progress and measure performance—is critical to the success of any AW venture. As Karen Sansone, director of alternative workplace solutions for Lucent Technologies, puts it, "You must get down to basics. Is there a deliverable? How do you know whether the employee or department has done something of value? For some types of employees, performance is clearly measurable. For others, it isn't. While considering different groups for remote work, managers realize that they need both to improve their understanding of what their people are doing and to focus on productivity. Remote work forces managers to think hard about the purpose and results of each job."

Once objectives and measures are in place, the management challenge becomes adapting to a new style of working. Sansone continues, "Remote management is really about a different form of communication. For example, if an employee in a traditional workplace is having difficulty achieving an objective, he or she could pop into the manager's office and say 'I have a problem. I need your help.' Or as a manager, you'd be checking in with them anyway. In a virtual office, people learn different methods. In conventional offices, employees sometimes wait at the door to catch their supervisors for a quick meeting. That's a waste of time you don't come across in the virtual office. What's more, the virtual-office manager and employee set agendas for their conversations so that both are better prepared."

Sansone and other managers agree that some direct contact is essential in the alternative workplace. "Performance evaluation and salary reviews must be done face to face," says Sansone. "So much of the managers' impact comes from sensitivity to individual reactions and the ability to gauge body language as well as words—reactions that simply are impossible to interpret over the phone or through E-mail."

Managers in an AW environment, particularly one in which employees work from a distance, must also pay close attention to time management. When employees are in the office only once a week or several times a month, it is critical that their time is not wasted. In a conventional office, changing the time or the day of a meeting at the last minute may be inconvenient for employees; in a virtual office, it may disrupt their work plans for the entire day, or worse.

Equally important are the peer relationships—so critical to any career—that flourish automatically in the conventional office but could atrophy in the alternative workplace. Joel W. Ratekin, a director of the virtual-office program at American Express, describes the employee's dilemma: "It's a natural response for a manager to grab anyone who is sitting around the office to put out a fire. The remote worker may be even more effective because he may be more focused and might be able to devote more hours to the problem. But for that person to lead or be part of the team, the manager has to think of contacting him." One AmEx unit uses a buddy system in which remote workers have on-site colleagues with whom they must talk every morning. What the employees talk about is up to them. The idea is to keep the remote worker in the loop by encouraging informal chats about new customers, product ideas, job transitions, office policies—the very topics that engage people around the water cooler in a conventional office.

Train for culture as well as technique. So much is new and different about the alternative workplace that managers must reeducate people about what used to be intuitive aspects of office life: when they should work, how often they should communicate, whether to talk or type, and what to say when they do. From an early age, we learn how to live in organizations at particular locations. In the alternative workplace, we have to learn to be in and of the organization while not being at it; at the same time, we have to differentiate our work and family lives while we're at home. Savvy leaders understand that organizational culture cannot be taken for granted in

In the alternative workplace, managers and employees have to learn how to be in *and* of *the organization while not being* at *it.*

the alternative workplace because people are not physically together to create it. But in practice, it is not easy to create or maintain an office culture in certain AW formats—for example, when managers

and the people they manage rarely meet face to face. Nor is it easy to figure out how much, or how little, a manager should be involved in helping employees balance the boundaries between work and home life.

Merrill Lynch runs a telecommuting lab to acclimate candidates for the alternative workplace before they formally adopt the new style of working. After extensive prescreening, employees spend two weeks at work in a simulated home office. Installed in a large room equipped with workstations in their conventional office building, prospective telecommuters communicate with their managers, customers, and colleagues solely by phone and E-mail. If they don't like this way of working, they can drop out and return to their usual workplace. To date, nearly 400 people have successfully moved from the simulation lab to their own home offices. The lab has proved a viable way to minimize the risks of placing people in the alternative workplace.

All the organizations I've cited have developed extensive training materials and techniques to suit their particular needs and situations. AT&T's James stresses the basics in a "survival training" course: How do I reserve work space? How do I route the phone and pager? How do I access the database? These companies also use rituals to teach new norms to AW participants—particularly those who will be working from home. Lucent's rituals include such simple tasks as writing to-do lists, dressing for work, giving dependents a good-bye kiss when "leaving" for the office at the beginning of the workday, then tidying up the desk, forwarding calls, shutting down the computer, and watching the evening news at the end of the day. These rituals replace traditional office routines such as morning conversations, coffee breaks, even the commute itself. They also create the breaks between home and work that help maintain a balance. Lucent's Sansone, herself a full-time "home officer," believes that such rituals are critically important for telecommuters because they link the traditions of the conventional office to the new realities of the home office.

Similarly, AW employees adapt to "telework" by creating rituals to suit their new schedules. One Lucent office has established a Wednesday morning doughnut club where virtual-office salespeople drop in for chatter and coffee. They used to meet informally at the water cooler to talk about particularly rewarding sales or problems with customers. Now, Sansone says, they think in advance about what they want to share with the group and the kind of feedback they need. AT&T's James has designed a café at one drop-in facility to encourage "casual collisions": those spontaneous encounters that occur where people gather and communicate. "We also have upholstered chairs with fold-down tables that go across your lap so you can work at them," she says. "It's a different environment—like being back in college."

Educate customers and other stakeholders. Don't expect customers, suppliers, and other stakeholders to understand your new work system immediately. Just as employees need time to ramp up, so too do your outside partners. They must be given the information and the time to adjust. So before launching an AW initiative, let customers and other stakeholders know what is going on. Explain how the new way of working may affect their contact with the organization, stress the benefits they stand to gain from the change, and be patient.

David Russell, a client marketing representative for IBM, says that his customers took a bit of time to adjust but notes that now communication is more efficient than ever: "I'm not in the office as much, so it's more difficult to reach me in person right away. Initially, I think customers found that frustrating. But now they realize that I'm never more than a few minutes away from voice mail and that I can return calls fairly quickly. Many of them are in similar situations; so we communicate a lot more by voice mail. And people have learned that if they don't reach me in person, they should leave a very specific message about the nature of their call so that I can start satisfying their needs immediately rather than playing phone tag."

AW employees must draw a firm line between their home and work lives—and be confident that the line is in the right place.

Keep an eye on how participants balance their work lives with their home lives. If one of the key reasons you are implementing an AW program is to attract and retain employees who will add the most value to your organization, then you must ensure that they are capable of handling the balance between their work lives and their personal lives. Doing so requires a good deal of honesty on both sides. In large part, the solution lies in the employee's ability to draw the line between work and home and to be confident that the line is in the right place.

Two questions on IBM's survey of its AW employees are "How well are you balancing your workload and personal life?" and "Does the company foster an environment that allows you to do that?" As Brad Geary, an IBM techline sales specialist, says, "Even if the company fosters such an environment, the real question is, How well are *you* doing? One of my teammates is in San Diego, and at lunchtime, he goes running on the beach. But he feels guilty that he's out enjoying himself during that part of the day. The company can emphasize the message that as long as it's made up for in some other way and you're still meeting your objectives, it's okay. But the employee has to believe it."

Jeffrey Hill, a project manager for IBM Global Employee Research, agrees that the responsibility belongs both to the company and to the individual. Hill lives in Logan, Utah, and telecommutes with internal clients throughout the country. He reports to an executive in New York whom he sees only several times a year. He says, "It's really about a change in mind-set. When I read the write-in comments on employee surveys, those who have been successful in mobility are really glowing about 'coaching my daughter's soccer team at 3:30 in the afternoon' or 'eating breakfast with my family for the first time in 15 years at IBM.' But then there are others who say, 'I'm always at work. I have my electronic leash. I'm never free.'"

What can be done in the corporate culture to help support a healthy balance? "We get a lot of suggestions that we should avoid highlighting Lou Gerstner's habit of bringing suitcases of work home with him every night," Hill jokes. But as he points out, the true solution lies in an ongoing effort by both the employee and the company to offer positive reinforcement continually, until and beyond the point where both sides are comfortable with the new work arrangement.

O RGANIZATIONS TODAY are poised on the edge of a new frontier: the alternative workplace offers a profound opportunity to benefit both the individual and the enterprise. But beyond one frontier lies another—what one might call a *mobility paradox.* IBM's Dayton explains, "We talk about mobility, but the next frontier is lack of mobility. The alternative workplace—and all the technology that enables it—is changing the way people collaborate." Indeed, we are moving from an era in which people seek connections with one another to an era in which people will have to decide when and where to disconnect—both electronically and socially. Organizations that pursue AW initiatives—particularly those with home office arrangements—must be mindful of that paradox. For only those organizations that balance individual and corporate interests will realize the concept's full potential.

Myths About the Alternative Workplace

MANY EXECUTIVES AND EMPLOYEES hold firm—but false—beliefs about the alternative workplace. These myths may dissuade organizations from exploring the potential benefits of AW initiatives.

The alternative workplace is for everyone.

IT ISN'T. Some high-tech advocates promote this notion, but it is clear that many people and functions today simply are not suited to the alternative workplace. The United States is perhaps a generation away from the threshold of broad-based computer literacy and systems integration that will enable the majority of people to be comfortable working outside the traditional office if they choose to do so. Yet leading organizations, such as those cited in this article, have shown that the AW concept applies to a large and growing segment of the workforce. Ironically, in this new paradigm, the youngest are the most skilled, the oldest are the most awestruck, and the middle-aged are the most resistant to the changes in mind-set and rituals that the alternative workplace requires.

An AW program can spearhead the process of organizational change.

IT CAN'T. Although an AW initiative can leverage reengineering and change-management efforts in the traditional workplace, it cannot launch them. Certain basic improvements must be made first—specifically, simplifying the organization, redesigning business processes, broadening access to information, and defining corporate performance measures. Otherwise, the AW initiative will be swamped by the sheer weight of these changes. But once the tide of change has begun to roll, AW employees can become strong advocates for extending the initiative throughout the organization. After all, they are already self-motivated, relatively autonomous, and results oriented. So they have the most to gain and the least to lose from influencing their peers to accept and adapt to AW work.

A company office is the most productive place to work.

NOT NECESSARILY. What few managers realize—but the alternative workplace highlights—is that the atmosphere and norms of the conventional office can distract people from their work. In a study of one well-managed office, these distractions averaged 70 minutes in an eight-hour day. Employees in the alternative workplace are usually more productive than their traditional counterparts because they learn how to juggle priorities and minimize downtime by making phone calls, writing E-mail, clearing accounts, and performing numerous other routine tasks during the short pockets of time between other commitments throughout the day. But AW employees also are hampered by home and office designs. Developers are just beginning to include quiet, private office space and robust electronics in new homes. Similarly, some new office buildings now include efficient "plug-and-play" drop-in space.

AW employees can take care of themselves.

NOT EXACTLY. It is naïve to think that all one needs is a laptop and a cellular phone to be effective in the alternative workplace. Most people need coaching in the basic protocols of AW life. And everyone needs direct access to the systems, gadgets, and technical support that enable remote work. A person's ability to excel in the alternative workplace depends on an array of new skills in communication, navigation, and leadership that takes time to learn and requires proactive, top-down support. Informal but essential social processes that occur spontaneously in the conventional workplace, such as the brown-bag lunch and the weekly happy hour, need to be managed in the alternative workplace.

The alternative workplace undermines teamwork and organizational cohesion.

IN FACT, it can build them—but in an unorthodox manner. Modern theories of teamwork are based on traditional, face-to-face models in which communication, information, and personal chemistry are intertwined in one location most or all of the time. In the alternative workplace, these links are unlocked. Technology empowers everyone—not just managers—wherever they are by enabling immediate communication with teammates and shared access to information. The chemistry within teams also has different elements. Contributions are defined more by content than by cosmetics when the team works electronically: an objective, egalitarian quality that often is missing in the conventional workplace. And relationships are enriched when managers use "face time" to focus on personal concerns rather than on business tasks.

The alternative workplace is really about computers.

IT'S NOT. The impetus for adopting an AW program is rooted in corporate strategy and renewal more than it is in technology. In a farsighted vision of its business, the U.S. Army is rethinking the fundamentals of its traditional workplace through a high-tech "digitized battlefield" supported by a virtual infrastructure of knowledge, training, and logistics. Similarly, in other organizations, the alternative workplace is really about rethinking the basics: What is the real purpose of your workplace? What work is performed? Who does it? How do they add value? What are their most important needs in the workplace? Where, when, and what types of facilities and systems do they require? How best can you provide them?

AT&T's First Shared Office

RICHARD S. MILLER, vice president of global services (GS) at AT&T, leads some 2,000 sales and support professionals serving major corporations and government clients in the eastern United States. His organization generates $4 billion in annual revenues; its expense budget is about $200 million, of which real estate represents 6%.

In December 1996, Miller learned on a television newscast about a competitor's initiative to pursue an AW program. Driven into action, he asked the help of AT&T's global real estate (GRE) organization in developing a new facility. His idea: a shared office that staff members who spend much of their time with customers outside the office would use as needed, without having assigned workstations. The objective: creating an environment in which teamwork would flourish while reducing real estate costs.

The GRE unit, then in the early stages of developing AT&T's Creative Workplace Solutions strategy, had not yet planned the type of facility Miller envisioned. So he and GRE's planning director, Thomas A. Savastano, Jr., formed a team to consider the alternatives. The team rejected several scenarios. One would have refitted a building already occupied by Miller's group, but that would have disrupted existing operations. Instead, the team opted for a three-part plan: redesign vacant AT&T space in Morristown, New Jersey, as a shared office; move 200 employees from five traditional office locations and 25 others from three satellite offices to the new facility; and redeploy the space to be vacated.

The total group included 58 salespeople, 101 technical specialists, and 66 management and support staff. Miller knew that the staff would need full-time space in the new facility. But he estimated that at least 60% of the sales and technical people would be out of the office with customers at any given time and therefore could share work space. At the time, the GS organization was beginning to transform its technical specialists into *virtual resources;* that is, rather than dedicating individuals to specific customers, these individuals would float from one account to another as needed. That change, Miller reflects, eased the transition from a conventional to an alternative workplace.

The new shared office works as follows: Through their laptops, employees log onto a system to reserve a workstation either before they arrive at the building or when they enter the lobby. Once there, they retrieve their own mobile file cabinet and wheel it to their reserved space. The workstations are six feet square and are arranged in pairs with a C-shaped work surface so that two people can work apart privately or slide around to work side by side. The reservation system routes employees' personal phone numbers to their reserved space. As one occupant says of the new arrangement, "I don't know who is going to sit next to me tomorrow, but interacting with different people all the time helps me think about customer issues more productively. I'm always getting a new perspective and new ideas from others' experience."

AT&T has installed three low-tech features in addition to its high-tech systems. A café encourages people to mingle for coffee and conversation about new sales, customer solutions, and office events. Two large chalkboards allow people to leave messages for others; this feature also reduces the paper flow within the office. And three types of enclosed space—phone rooms, "personal harbors," and team rooms—accommodate private meetings and teleconferences.

AT&T's project shows how significant the tangible and intangible results of an AW initiative can be. It cost $2.1 million to develop, including construction, furniture, equipment, and systems. But the investment was well worth the effort, as the accompanying table shows. Annual savings alone amount to more than $460,000, or $2,000 per person. Over five years, the company will avoid nearly $2 million in costs associated with running a traditional office. In addition, individual space was

Shared Office Metrics in Morristown

	Before	After
Square feet	45,000	27,000
Annual rent	$1.2M	$0.7M
Five-year expense[1]	$6.4M	$4.5M
Five-year after-tax NPV	$1.9M	$1.2M
Annual rent per square foot	$26	$26
Persons	196	225
Square feet per person	230	120
Annual rent per person	$6,100	$3,100
Annual telecom cost per person	$10,600	$11,200
Total project cost[2]	NA	$2.1M
Total project cost per square foot[2]	NA	$79
Total project cost per person[2]	NA	$9,500
Annual savings	NA	$463,500

Notes:
Figures in the table have been rounded.
1. This metric includes recurring voice and data charges; without recurring costs, "After" is $3.9M.
2. This metric includes total construction, furniture, voice and data installation, and training and systems costs.

halved, and team-meeting space doubled. Finally, the project has produced closer teamwork, better customer service, and greater employee satisfaction.

How Senior Executives at American Express View the Alternative Workplace

Richard Karl Goeltz is vice chairman and chief financial officer, and David House is president of Establishment Services Worldwide at American Express. Goeltz has overall responsibility for corporate real estate at AmEx and is a sponsor of the company's AW initiatives. When House joined AmEx in 1993, his division launched a virtual-office strategy in its field offices and has recently completed a similar pilot project at its headquarters. Here, the two sum up some of the salient considerations for managers who are assessing the pros and cons of AW initiatives.

On the benefits of an AW program, Goeltz comments:

THE BENEFITS CAN BE REALIZED in terms of customers, employees, and shareholders. In terms of customers, if a company has a sophisticated, highly efficient network for communications and data manipulation—an essential component of a broad-based virtual-office initiative—then its employees should be able to respond more fully and more promptly to customer needs ranging from simple inquiries to more complex product demands. In terms of staff, we've found that we can draw from a broader pool of people because our employees can be in many locations. Through virtual-office programs, we might be able to attract people with proven records of success who can't or won't move to our office sites. If we can say to such qualified people, "We can offer you a stimulating, rewarding, well-compensated position, and you can work at home," then that is good for the company and for the economy. In terms of shareholders, if a company is giving its customers better service and is realizing savings on real estate and so forth, then naturally there are substantial shareholder benefits.

House underscores the potential:

HERE'S AN EXAMPLE of someone the company would have lost had we not been flexible in our work arrangements. A manager in one of our divisions was going to leave the company when her boss asked me if she could take an open position in our Chicago office but live in Michigan. I told him, "If she's the right candidate, she can live anywhere." She now goes to Chicago several times a month. When I talk with her on the phone, I don't know whether she's in Chicago or Michigan. She travels a fair amount of the time anyway, so it really doesn't matter where she lives. This is a quality-of-life issue for the employee. But for the company, it's an issue of finding the best person for the job.

Goeltz continues:

THE QUESTION IS whether or not a virtual-office program dovetails with the kind of business a company does—whether it can serve an operational need or help improve performance. There are particular opportunities in financial services businesses like ours because our business is information. But each case—indeed, each department or division—must be considered separately.

The two managers agree that getting people to adjust to new ways of working is a major hurdle. Goeltz says:

CONSIDER THE MANAGER who is accustomed to walking into a traditional office and seeing 50 people. In the virtual office, midlevel managers relinquish direct, visual employee supervision. The key difference is that in an information industry, productivity is monitored through electronic systems, whether or not the manager is on site. How many calls does an employee handle? How well and how quickly? If a supervisor periodically wants to listen in on a conversation to determine how a customer representative is handling a call, it doesn't make any difference whether that supervisor is in the next office or halfway around the world, barring time zone considerations. You don't have to be physically present to monitor productivity, efficiency, and quality of customer service. But it is extremely difficult to change the mind-set that really wants that presence.

House concurs, noting that the change is equally challenging from the employee's viewpoint:

IT TAKES DISCIPLINE and confidence for people to feel good about this and say, "Look, I'm going to telecommute. I'm going to work at home two or three days a week, and I'm going to come in here for meetings only twice a week." People have the feeling that if they're not in the office—if they're not seen—they'll be overlooked. One of the ways to overcome that is to encourage telecommuting at senior levels of the organization and let the rest of the company see how it works. I really believe that acceptance of the virtual office is mainly a question of leadership—taking a position and showing that it's now part of our culture.

Goeltz stresses the difference between encouragement and force:

IT IS DANGEROUS, at best, for senior management to mandate an AW scenario. What one has to do is to demonstrate the benefits that can be achieved from virtual-office concepts, satellite offices, and other arrangements that share the same principles. When the benefits are clear—be they cost reduction, improved customer service, or reduced commuting times—then people will be more likely to embrace the new way of working.

House observes that participants should understand the advantages and the limitations of the alternative workplace:

THE VIRTUAL OFFICE is not, and should not be, an all-or-nothing scenario. For example, it is far more difficult to have a brainstorming meeting over the phone, because you can't have the same give-and-take and you can't read body language. And yet it is also critical to understand that time spent in the central office—in the presence of colleagues—is not the same as it used to be. In the virtual office, if employees come to a meeting, it is for a particular purpose. Something has to be accomplished, or else the time has been wasted. In the traditional office, a group of people might meet to *discuss* a certain issue. In the virtual office, when people meet, they should *decide* the issue. In the virtual office, the old adage "Time is money" is taken to a new level: time is money, satisfaction, balance, performance, and a host of other things as well.

Originally published in May–June 1998
Reprint 98301

A Second Career

The Possible Dream

HARRY LEVINSON

Executive Summary

WHAT MANAGER HASN'T sat at his desk on a gloomy
Monday morning wondering what he was doing there
and asking himself whether he could make it as the skip-
per of a charter boat in the Bahamas or as the operator
of a ski resort in Colorado? Sometimes he dreams of
becoming a lawyer, sometimes, simply of writing a book.
Regardless of the dream itself, however, managers need
to satisfy a few conditions, this author says, before they
can be sure that their choice of a second career is a
wise one and not simply a flight from the routine and frustration that is common to all jobs. First managers need to
understand their "ego ideals," their hidden images of
how they would like to be. Then they need to determine
how they prefer to behave in certain situations—whether,
for instance, they prefer risk taking on their own or the
security of groups. Armed with an understanding of their

own visions and behavior patterns, managers are in a
position to weigh their career options realistically.

J UST TWO YEARS after his appointment as director
of marketing services, 35-year-old Tom Conant started
thinking about leaving his job and enrolling in law
school. He had fantasies of addressing the bench in an
attempt to persuade the judge to side with his position.
Tom imagined how it would feel to demolish the
opposing lawyer by asking the witness penetrating
questions that led inexorably to the conclusion he
sought. He couldn't wait to get started.

Tom had joined the company right after business
school and in 12 years there had topped one success with
another. His marketing acumen, his ability to innovate,
do research, and carry through new programs brought
the company important new business. In other respects,
too, Tom had been a model manager to his superiors and
his subordinates. He was marked as a comer. Tom's ini-
tial impatience to sink his teeth into new challenges had
posed some problems, but as he received new responsibilities, Tom began to relax and seemed to enjoy his
work and his colleagues.

When he found himself thinking of a career in law,
Tom surprised himself. He had thought that he might be
wooed by competitors, but he had never expected to
think of abandoning his career. Leo Burns, Tom's prede-
cessor as manager of marketing services and his mentor,
hoped to see his protégé follow him to the vice presi-
dency. Tom knew that his resignation would shatter Leo,
and that knowledge annoyed him. He didn't want to
fight or disappoint Leo.

Anger at Leo slowly mounted. In his fantasy Tom tried to explain to Leo his reasons for leaving, to describe the soul-searching he had done in the last year, but Leo wouldn't listen. He pictured Leo's disappointment turning to irritation. The imaginary drama came to a climax with Leo insisting that Tom leave the company immediately. "Marketing doesn't need you!" Tom imagined Leo shouting. "Just get on with your plans and get out!"

When Tom had these fantasies, he always had second thoughts about making such a move. He had a good career ahead of him. He was a loyal company person, and the company had been good to him. His recent promotion had given him new responsibilities and a reputation in the industry. And he hadn't really been that bored for the last two years.

Yet in calmer moments Tom remembered other managers who had switched careers. An engineer he knew had left a responsible job in product development at the age of 40 to go to law school and was now a patent attorney. He boasted that it was a change he was glad he had made: "I was going to spend the rest of my life putting new faces on old products. Now I can use what I know about engineering to help people who are going to make real changes happen."

Tom reflected also about the many people in the news who were on their second, or even third, careers. California ex-governor Jerry Brown had been a Jesuit seminarian before entering politics; Henry Kissinger had been a professor before becoming a diplomat. Several business school deans had been CEOs, and university presidents have become business executives.

As always, Tom concluded his reverie with a farewell handshake; he was leaving his old friends behind. He imagined them thinking that they, too, should have undertaken second careers.

Almost everyone at some point thinks of a second career. Many people have good reasons. Tom's law school fantasy was based in part on a cool assessment of his own life and the contemporary business situation. He believed that growing consumer movements would force the marketing field to change radically in the next decade. Despite their temporary relaxation, he thought that federal, state, and local regulations controlling advertising and promotion would increase. By combining his marketing experience with a law school education, Tom reasoned he could steal a march on this trend and build a solid future for himself either as an in-house counsel or as a consultant.

As the years pass, most people—regardless of their professions or skills—find their jobs or careers less interesting, stimulating, or rewarding. By midlife, many feel the need for new and greener occupational fields. They yearn for opportunities to reassert their independence and maturity and to express the needs and use the talents of a different stage of life.

Some people feel they are no longer in the running for advancement, some that their talents and skills are not being fully used, and some that they have outgrown their jobs, companies, or disciplines. Others, feeling blocked by being in the wrong company, industry, or position, are bored. Some are in over their heads, while others had merely drifted into their jobs or chosen directions prematurely. One or a combination of these feelings can make a person hate to go to work in the morning and can trigger thoughts of a way out.

The realities of contemporary organizational life also stimulate a manager to think about a second career: the competition is stiffer every year. Even to the young manager, the accelerating pace of change makes obsolescence a threat. Rapid technological changes (which demand higher levels of education and training), more differentiated markets, and unpredictable economic circumstances all make it improbable that a manager will have a life-long career in one field or one organization.

By their middle or late 30s, managers usually know how far their careers will take them. By comparing his promotion rate to those of peers, a manager can tell if he has leveled off. If a manager's latest assignment takes him out of the organization's prescribed route to the top, the upward movement probably has ended.

Other factors behind the wish for second careers are the effects aging and growth have on people. Although an intense period of skills training, job rotation, long hours of overtime, and much traveling may have satisfied them when they were younger and just beginning their careers, managers as they get older probably find the pace exhausting and the rewards insufficiently attractive to compensate for the loss of other gratifications.

But the reasons for thinking about a second career are not always positive. Some people want to change because they are always dissatisfied with themselves; some are depressed and angry; some have anxiety about death that induces restlessness; and some have overvalued themselves and believe they are more talented or capable than they really are. Some managers can't tolerate bosses. Others think they should have been CEO a long time ago. Some are unwilling to acquire experience, while others are competing with old classmates. Some are just competing—and not as well as they'd like.

Seeking a new career for these reasons is an exercise in futility. If a manager blames the job, the boss, or the company when the source of his discontent is really himself, his second career is likely to be as disappointing as his first. Therefore a manager, before embarking on choosing a second career, must have an honest picture of himself and understand the changes he probably will go through.

Stages in Adult Development

As middle age approaches, thoughts about a second career intensify.[1] Building on the work of Sigmund Freud, psychoanalyst Erik H. Erikson has outlined three stages of adulthood: intimacy, generativity, and integrity.[2] Each stage has a psychosocial crisis and each has its task.

The first adult stage, intimacy, which lasts from about age 21 to age 35, is the most spontaneously creative period. It is an innovative and productive time. The young adult channels great energies into choosing and launching a career and, usually, into contracting a marriage and establishing a family. The third and final stage, integrity, begins at approximately age 55. Ideally, at this age a person ties together his life experience and comes to terms with his life. At work, he prepares for retirement and reflects on his career.

In between, during the stage of generativity, from about age 35 to age 55, the adult lays the foundations for the next generation. Commonly called the mid-life transition, this is the time of reevaluation. At home, the children are leaving the nest and husbands and wives have to rethink their relationship to each other. At work, the drive to compete and excel is peaking, and executives pay more attention to bringing other, younger managers along.

The transition between intimacy and generativity is, according to Daniel Levinson, the time during which the adult makes his last assertion for independence.[3] Levinson calls this "the BOOM [becoming one's own man] effect." His studies of executives indicate that at about age 37, the adult throws off the guidance or protection of older mentors or managers and takes full charge of himself. Those that are able to make this last stand for independence go on to new heights. They demand more responsibility or start their own companies. Others either don't assert themselves or are rejected when they make demands. The BOOM effect is an impetus for seeking a new career.

In our culture people have opportunities to do many things. In youth they choose one and leave the others behind, but they promise themselves they'll come back to them. Fifteen years out of school, people tend to feel satiated with what they're doing—even if it is something with high status and high pay—and itch to fulfill old promises to themselves. They tend to become restless when circumstances keep them from doing so and become dismayed when they realize that they can't go back and start all over again.

When people are in this stage of life, they need to seek counsel, to talk at length about their reasons, and to listen to others' experiences and perceptions. They also need the support of others who are important to them through this difficult decision-making and transition period. Such assistance can ensure that the manager will make a sound second-career choice rather than flee impulsively from frustration or boredom. It might even result in a wise decision on the part of a promising executive to remain, with renewed enthusiasm, in his organization. A manager who thinks through the issues of a second career also readies himself to help others with the same concerns.

Who Are You?

The most critical factor for people to consider in choosing a gratifying second career is their ego ideal. It can serve as a road map. Central to a person's aspirations, the ego ideal is an idealized image of oneself in the future. It includes the goals people would like to achieve and how they would like to see themselves. At an early age, children identify with parents and other power figures, find out how to please or resist them, and learn to adapt to feeling small and helpless in comparison with them. How they do these things, as well as other unconscious factors, determines how their ego ideals develop. During childhood and adolescence, the young person incorporates rising aspirations built on academic or career achievements into the ego ideal and, as time goes on, also includes successive models, each of which has a more specialized competence.

Throughout life people strive toward their ego ideals, but no one ever achieves it. With successive accomplishments, aspirations rise. But as people feel they are progressing toward their ego ideals, their self-pictures are more rather than less positive. The closer a person gets to the ego ideal, therefore, the better he feels about himself. The greater the gap between one's ego ideal and one's current self-image, the angrier one is at oneself and the more inadequate, guilty, and depressed one feels.

When a career helps satisfy the ego ideal, life and work are rewarding and enjoyable. When a career does not help meet these self-demands, work is a curse. In short, the wish to attain the ego ideal, to like oneself, is the most powerful of motivating forces. Delivery on the promises one makes to oneself is an important aspect of choosing a new direction.

TAPPING INTO THE EGO IDEAL

Because people begin to form their ego ideals in earliest childhood, developing an accurate understanding of them is difficult. A careful review of family history and school and work experiences can go along way in outlining the needs that are important to the ego ideal. A manager can help the process along by discussing with a listener or a friend answers to the following questions (although this exercise may strike you as off the point, there are very good reasons for carrying it out):

1. What were your father's or father substitute's values? Not what did your father say or do, but what did he stand for? What things were important to him? What was the code he lived by? And then, what were your mother's values?

2. What was the first thing you did that pleased your mother? Small children try hard to please their mothers, who are the most important figures in their lives. Every child's earliest efforts to please mother become ingrained behavior. They are, therefore, a significant part of each person's characteristic way of behaving and have an important influence on subconscious goals. Later, children try to please the father, too. (Sometimes, especially for women, it may be the mother's values that are more important and the activities that pleased father that weigh more heavily.)

3. Who were your childhood heroes or heroines? Did you idolize athletes, movie stars, or political figures?

What kind of people do you now enjoy reading about or watching on TV? What kind of achievements do you admire?

4. Who are and were your models—relatives, teachers, scoutmasters, preachers, bosses, characters in stories? What did they say or do that made you admire them?

5. When you were able to make choices, what were they? What elective subjects did you take in high school? What major did you pursue in college? What jobs have you accepted? At first glance, these choices may seem to have been random, but they were not. And when you take a retrospective look at them, a pattern emerges.

6. What few experiences in your lifetime have been the most gratifying? Which gave you the greatest pleasure and sense of elation? The pleasure you took in the experience was really the pleasure you took in yourself. What were you doing?

7. Of all the things you've done, at which were you the most successful? What were you doing and how were you doing it?

8. What would you like your epitaph or obituary to say? What would you like to be remembered for? What would you like to leave as a memorial?

The answers to these questions will help managers sketch the outlines of their ego ideals and give them a sense of the main thrust of their lives.

If you still have some doubts about direction after you've talked these questions through, you might take a battery of psychological tests to complement the definition of your ego ideal. Many counseling psychologists provide interest, aptitude, and values inventories as well as tests of intelligence, reasoning, and other capacities. They can interpret the test results and advise you about their significance for your career choice.

How Do You Like to Act?

The next step is to determine the kinds of occupational activities that fit the way you like to behave, how you like to do your job or deal with coworkers. The point here is to determine whether you are temperamentally fit for the job you're thinking of moving to. For instance, Tom in the opening vignette had always wanted to take on new responsibilities and challenges and to act alone taking risks rather than in a group, where interdependence is important. If Tom decided to go to law school to become a consultant working on his own, he would be making a choice consistent with how he worked best. He would be choosing an environment in which he would be psychologically comfortable.

In determining how your personality will fit with a job, a listener's or friend's questions and insights will be valuable. Explore the following areas:

How do you handle aggressive energy? Do you channel it into the organization and administration of projects? Are you reluctant to express it? For instance, do you have difficulty taking people to task or confronting colleagues or subordinates? How do you react when someone challenges your opinion?

Channeling aggressive energy into the organization and administration of projects means that the person can comfortably take charge and can focus his

achievement effort into organizational achievement
rather than personal aggrandizement. A person who is
reluctant to express his aggression may have difficulty
speaking up at the right time or representing himself
adequately or analyzing problems and discussions with
other people. Difficulty in taking people to task or confronting colleagues is also a product of reluctance to
express aggression and usually reflects a good deal of
underlying unconscious guilt.

A person who is unable to take people to task cannot
take charge as a manager; and one who is unable to confront others cannot give colleagues or subordinates honest performance appraisals.

How do you handle affection? Some people prefer to
be independent, while others enjoy working closely with
people. Do you need constant approval and encouragement or does the quality of your work satisfy you? Can
you praise others or do you find it difficult to express
positive feelings?

While some people enjoy the affectionate interchange
and camaraderie of working closely with others, some
people prefer to be independent. The latter may either
deny their need for other people's praise, approval, and
affection or simply feel more comfortable keeping a
distance.

Many managers have great difficulty telling others
when they do good work. It is as if any expression of
emotion is difficult for them. For some, this is a matter of
conscience: they feel like hypocrites for praising work
that isn't outstanding. For others, praise may seem to
invite a closer relationship with the person being praised
or may violate the picture of stoic self-control they want
to present.

How do you handle dependency? Do you have
trouble making decisions without your manager's OK?
Do you work better when you're in charge or in a number
2 position? Do you work as well independently as on a
team? Do you have difficulty asking for and using the
help of others?

Although most of us fear becoming helplessly dependent on others, in organizations we are necessarily
dependent on a lot of other people to get our work done.
But some people can't tolerate this aspect of themselves.
They need to do everything on their own. It is all right for
other people to lean on them, and indeed sometimes
they encourage it, but it is not all right for them to lean
on other people. Such people disdain others' advice or
guidance, even when seeking professional help is appropriate.

On the other hand, some people do well only when
they can lean on somebody else's guidance or direction
and panic when they don't have that. And while some
people may work well by themselves, they may not
accept other people's needs to depend on them. Such
people will not be good bosses.

Listeners' or friends' special knowledge of a manager's
working habits will enable them to be perceptive in
questioning the manager in these areas. In addition, the
manager should ask others—friends, co-workers,
colleagues—to share with him their perceptions of his
characteristic behavior. Sometimes they can tell the
manager about working habits that he himself is not
aware of. For instance, over a period of time friends
might have noticed that Tom, from the opening vignette,
enjoyed bearing full responsibility and risk for a project
and making it work through his own expertise. This

information could help Tom choose whether to join a company as in-house counsel or to become an independent consultant. A friend could point out that given his characteristic working style, Tom would probably enjoy the latter better.

In some cases, of course, friends may not be very perceptive or may have their own interests at heart and not be very helpful. At times like these, managers should definitely seek professional help.

Which Way to Go?

Armed with an understanding of his ego ideal and working style, the manager is now ready to weigh options more wisely. He may choose to launch a second career or he may decide to stick with his course in the organization. Whatever his decision, his friends' support and his deeper understanding of himself and his motivation will equip him to attack his chosen career with new dedication and enthusiasm.

Second careers are evolutionary. They stem from some interest that has lain dormant or has been abandoned in favor of another occupation. Asked if he had any idea of what he wanted to do when he left the chairmanship of Dain, Kalman & Quail, an investment banking firm in Minneapolis, for a new vocation, Wheelock Whitney answered, "Yes, really. I thought I'd like to pursue some other things that I cared about." Among these interests was the Johnson Institute, a center studying and treating the chemically dependent. Whitney had become deeply involved in the institute eight years earlier when his wife was undergoing treatment for alcoholism.[4]

Many turn to second careers that extend a previous occupational thrust; they may go into business for themselves in fields they already know. By searching the past for those budding interests that had no chance to flower, a manager can draw a long list of career options. At the same time, a manager can eliminate those that are no longer interesting or pleasurable. In choosing his second career, William Damroth said he switched from the chairmanship of Lexington Corporation because "to me the main thing was that I couldn't continue doing what I enjoy the most, which is the creative role, the intense bringing together of all factors, saying, 'It ought to look like this.' For instance, what I'm doing today is much more satisfying than the long-range planning you have to do for a company. Today's satisfaction is immediate."[5]

After eliminating undesirable options, a manager should investigate what additional training is required for each of the remaining possibilities and how much he can afford to invest. To pick up some careers, managers need to spend years in full-time professional or academic training; others they can approach through a course of reading, night school, or correspondence study. By seeing how the remaining options fit with how he prefers to behave and by understanding his ego ideal, a manager can usually narrow the field to one or two general directions. At this point, a manager considering a career change should again ask a friend or counselor to act as a sounding board, letting the manager talk through options and refine his ideas.

Finally, before a manager makes a choice, he should consider a number of other critical issues:

Family. Whom do you have responsibility for—a mother-in-law, an uncle, a grandfather, a handicapped sister or brother? Do these responsibilities limit your options? Do your responsibilities to your spouse and children impose geographic or financial constraints?

Present job. If a manager comes to a premature judgment or acts impulsively, he risks leaving his present job thinking that the company left much to be desired. Will your peers and boss see the move as a rejection of the company and of your work together? Feeling abandoned, they might attack you. The possibility of anger and disappointment is especially high when you and your superior have worked closely together and when you respect and admire each other. Furthermore, some people, disappointed that they failed to act when the time was right, will be jealous. They may unload on you their anger with themselves. Are you prepared for these conflicts?

It will help you to think about what it means to lose these peers and mentors. Rather than thinking that you are being disloyal, recognize that people who prepare themselves for a second career are doing the organization as well as themselves a favor by making space for younger, talented managers looking forward to promotion.

Status. One's status in the community is directly related to one's status at work. Choosing another career may well result in changing one's status. How important is that to you? How important is it that you associate with the same people you have associated with before, that you play golf at the same clubs or take part in the same social activities? Because your spouse and children will also be affected, the family must discuss this issue together. The sacrifices may well be severe.

Rebuilding. If you're thinking of starting a new business or launching a new career, chances are that you will have to build a clientele. Rarely does a person move from one organization to another and take with him all of his accounts. For example, a lawyer told me that when he and his colleagues left a large firm to start their own, they expected their clients to follow them. Only a small fraction did, and the new firm had to build its clientele from scratch. Anyone starting his own business should expect it to take from two to five years to build a stable of customers.

Freedom versus constraints. For a mature manager in the BOOM period, the pressure to be autonomous, to do what he wants to do, to be free of commitments to somebody else, is very high. Therefore, in choosing an activity or direction, it is important to choose, insofar as you can, something that allows you maximum freedom to come and go, to do as you wish, while meeting the formal obligations of the role. As William Damroth comments: "My time is my own. I can lie on my back for two hours if I want. Instead of saying, 'This is what I want' and moving toward it, I've said 'This is what I don't like,' and I've eliminated it. I've cut away all the things that make life unhappy for me. I don't have any tension headaches in the mornings."[6]

But one doesn't always achieve freedom so easily. As we go through life we aspire to many things—promotions, new roles, different experiences. And we often ask ourselves, "Who am I to want to do that? What right do I have to seek that goal?" Self-critical feelings often prevent us from moving toward aspirations that we have every right to work toward and achieve.

The issue becomes particularly important with respect to a second career. Because a mature manager recognizes, if he hasn't before, that he has every right to pursue anything he wants to, now is the time to act. Anyone is eligible for any aspiration. One may not achieve it, but one has as much right as anybody else to want it and try for it.

Year-long depression. I have never seen a person make a significant career shift without experiencing a year-long depression. I don't mean that people are down in the dumps for a year but that they feel loss, ambivalence, and fear that things may not work out. Caught in an ambiguous situation in which they are not yet rooted, they feel detached from their stable routines.

The longer the manager has been with an organization, the more likely he has come to depend on it; the closer his relationships have been with his colleagues, the greater will be the sense of loss. The more his family has been tied to the organization, the more profound these feelings are likely to be.

Talk. All change is loss and all loss requires mourning.[7] Even when promoted, one loses the support of colleagues, friends, and known ways of doing things. To dissipate the inevitable sorrow, you have to turn it into words. To detach yourself from old ties and give up old habits, you have to talk about the experience. Feeling that they have to be heroic, some managers, men particularly, either deny that they are having such experiences or grit their teeth and try to plow through them. That way of acting doesn't deal with the depression; it only buries it and makes one vulnerable to physiological symptoms and over-reactions when traumas occur.

It is important to have somebody to talk to and to be able to talk to that person freely. But even with the most careful and sensitive support from spouse and friends, you may get sidetracked, spin your wheels and get stuck in the mire. If after such talk you are no clearer about your choice, it may be time to consult a professional. The issues and feelings any careful self-appraisal touches on are often too complex to examine or discuss without professional help.

Joint experiences. Husbands' and wives' careers often separate them. When one member of the marriage makes a career change, new problems having to do with adult development emerge. Early in a marriage the spouses go in different directions, the husband usually to earn a livelihood and the wife usually to bear children. After her child rearing is done, the wife may return to work, but chances are nevertheless that the two spouses will still go in different occupational directions. Their only common interest tends to be the children or family problems.

Usually by the time a person has reached midcareer, the children are out on their own or close to it. The spouses now have to talk to each other. But if they have gone in different directions, they may have trouble communicating. A second career can help spouses reunite. One couple, for example, became interested in antiques. Together they went to antique shows and searched for old glass. When they gave up their old careers, they decided to run an antique store together. What was originally a shared hobby gave the couple financial security while they worked together.

Sometimes a new career threatens an old relationship. One manager was successful and widely respected in his organization. Although unequal to him in status or earning power, his wife also had professional training. When they decided to have children, she left her job to rear them. During those years, he was a supportive helpmate. When she was able, she went to law school and subsequently entered a prestigious law firm.

Her status and income now exceed her husband's. He has taken a backseat to her and, with some feelings of embarrassment, carries on some of the household and family maintenance activities that she formerly handled. He speaks of his new situation with mingled pride and shame and is now considering a second career himself.

Open options. Even if you have exercised great care in choosing a second career, the change won't necessarily work out. Economic vagaries as well as factors that you couldn't foresee may cut your second career short. If you left your old job on a positive note, however, it may be possible to get it back. Many organizations recognize that a manager who has tested himself elsewhere and wants to return is likely to be an even better and more highly motivated employee.

Notes

1. See my article, "On Being a Middle-Aged Manager," HBR, July–August 1969, p. 57.

2. Erik H. Erikson, *Childhood and Society*, 2d ed. (New York: Norton, 1963).

3. Daniel Levinson, Charlotte N. Darrow, Edward B. Klein, Maria H. Levinson, and Braxton McKee, *The Seasons of a Man's Life* (New York: Alfred A. Knopf, 1978).

4. See "Don't Call It Early Retirement," HBR interview with Wheelock Whitney and William G. Damroth, HBR, September–October 1975, p. 103.

5. Ibid, p. 113.

6. Ibid, p. 118.

7. See my article, "Easing the Pain of Personal Loss," HBR, September–October 1972, p. 80.

Originally published in May–June 1983
Reprint 83307

Author's note: To avoid the ungainly use of his or her throughout this article I use him and his where it's not possible to make the reference plural.

About the Contributors

MAHLON APGAR IV was appointed by President Clinton as Assistant Secretary of the Army for Installations and Environment in June 1998. Prior to this position, he was a Real Estate Consultant and Principal at Apgar and Company; a Partner with McKinsey and Company; a Professor at the Harvard Graduate School of Design; and a Real Estate Executive at Wellington Management Company. Mr. Apgar is recognized as a leading expert on real estate, facilities, and infrastructure programs. The editor of two books, he has also published numerous articles on real estate management that appeared in *Harvard Business Review* and other professional journals.

FERNANDO BARTOLOMÉ is Professor of Management at the Instituto de Empresa in Madrid, and Visiting Professor at INSEAD in Fontainebleau, France. In addition to *Must Success Cost So Much?* he also authored *Basic Books 1981* (with Paul Evans). He has conducted research on work and life balance since 1968, and works as a consultant on this and other organizational behavior issues with many international companies in the United States, Europe, Latin America, and Asia.

PERRY CHRISTENSEN is a Senior Consultant at WFD Consulting. He has consulted with numerous companies in the area of work/life strategy, work redesign, and change management processes. Mr. Christensen joined WFD Consulting from Merck & Co. Inc., where he worked for 15 years in a variety of human resource executive positions and was responsible for designing and implementing many innovative human resource, diversity, and work/life policies. Mr. Christensen is a member of the Conference Board's Work and Life Leadership Council and conducts ongoing research in collaboration with the Wharton Business School on effective work/life strategies, management competencies, and change management processes. He has written several other articles and book chapters on work/life strategy and is the coeditor of *Integrating Work and Life: The Wharton Resource Guide.*

JESSICA DEGROOT is Founder and President of The Third Path Institute, a nonprofit organization dedicated to reshaping our model of family to enhance all employees' abilities to integrate work and other personal priorities across the life cycle. In addition to "Work and Life: The End of the Zero Sum Game," she is the coauthor of *Integrating Work and Life: The Wharton Resource Guide*, a training manual for teaching individuals and managers how to integrate work and personal life. Ms. DeGroot worked as coorganizer of the Wharton Work/Life Roundtable until spring 1998. Currently she teaches a graduate-level entrepreneurship class at the Wharton School of Business. She and her husband balance two children and two careers from their home offices in Philadelphia.

PAUL A. LEE EVANS is Professor of Organizational Behavior at INSEAD, Fontainebleau. His research and consulting focuses on international human resource management, and he is the coauthor of *Must Success Cost So Much?*, *Human Resource Management in International Firms*, and *The Globalization Challenge.*

STEWART D. FRIEDMAN is the Director of Ford Motor Company's Leadership Development Center. He is on leave from the Wharton School, where he is the Practice Professor of Management. He is the Founding Director of both the Wharton Leadership Program and the Wharton Work/Life Integration Project. Dr. Friedman worked for five years as a clinical psychologist and health care manager before earning his Ph.D. in organizational psychology. He has published several books and articles on work/life integration, leadership development, and the dynamics of individual and organizational change. His most recent book (with Jeff Greenhaus) is *Work and Family—Allies or Enemies?* He consults with a wide variety of public and private sector organizations and serves as an executive coach for individual clients.

MICHAEL S. KIMMEL is Professor of Sociology at SUNY at Stony Brook. He is the author of seven books including *The Politics of Manhood, Manhood: A Cultural History, Men's Lives,* and *The Gendered Society.* He is the editor for *Men and Masculinities,* an interdisciplinary scholarly journal, a book series on men and masculinity at the University of California Press, and the Sage Series on Men and Masculinities. He is the Spokesperson for the National Organization for Men Against Sexism (NOMAS) and lectures extensively on campuses in the United States and abroad.

At the time his article was first published, HARRY LEVINSON was Emeritus Professor of Psychiatry at the Harvard Medical School in Boston, Massachusetts, and chairman of the board of the Levinson Institute, a Boston-based consulting firm of psychiatrists and psychologists. He has been a frequent contributor to *Harvard Business Review.*

At the time her article was first published, FELICE N. SCHWARTZ was President and Founder of Cataylst, a nonprofit research and advisory organization that works with corporations to foster the career and leadership development of women.

Index